D1447667

WALKING ON RUM
AND THE SMALL ISLES

About the Author

Peter Edwards grew up in Sussex and nurtured a love of walking and mountain biking amid the 'blunt, bow-headed, whale-backed' hills of the South Downs. He has undertaken numerous walking and cycling expeditions in Europe and beyond and is particularly drawn to wild and remote landscapes. He lives in Glasgow with his wife, Fiona. Peter also writes about his walking and cycling trips on his blog at www.writesofway.com.

Other Cicerone guides by the author
Walking on Jura, Islay and Colonsay
Mountain Biking on the South Downs

WALKING ON RUM
AND THE SMALL ISLES

by Peter Edwards

2 POLICE SQUARE, MILNTHORPE, CUMBRIA LA7 7PY
www.cicerone.co.uk

© Peter Edwards
First edition 2012
ISBN: 978 1 85284 662 6

Printed by KHL Printing, Singapore

Dedication

*This book is dedicated to my father-in-law, Alex 'Alasdair Beag' Rintoul, a
proud Scotsman who loves his country – 'good gear comes in wee bulk'!*

Advice to Readers

While every effort is made by our authors to ensure the accuracy of guidebooks as they go to print, changes can occur during the lifetime of an edition. If we know of any, there will be an Updates tab on this book's page
on the Cicerone website (www.cicerone.co.uk), so please check before
planning your trip. We also advise that you check information about such
things as transport, accommodation and shops locally. Even rights of way
can be altered over time. We are always grateful for information about
any discrepancies between a guidebook and the facts on the ground, sent
by email to info@cicerone.co.uk or by post to Cicerone, 2 Police Square,
Milnthorpe LA7 7PY, United Kingdom.

Front cover: Dùn Mòr sea stack, Sanday, looking across the Sound of Canna to
the hills of Rum

CONTENTS

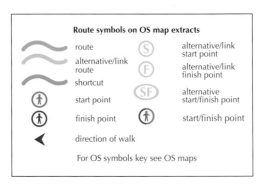

Acknowledgements

Thanks to all the team at Cicerone for transforming my words and pictures into a rather fine wee guidebook! While researching the routes for this guide I have enjoyed the excellent company of Kirsten Abingdon, Rich Baldwin, Sarah Blann, James Boulter (www.backpackingbongos.wordpress.com), Andy and Jen Dodd, Andy Godfrey, Giulia Hetherington, Clare Meadows, Fiona Rintoul and Dùghall Mòr nan Eilean. Thanks to Morar-based mountain leader, Peter Khambatta (www.adventurenevis.com) for several pictures. Thanks to Alex Munro and Bob McFarlane of www.blueskyscotland.blogspot.com for pictures and an inspirational eye on Scotland's great outdoors.

Thanks to Jura-based photographer, Konrad Borkowski for the red deer pictures (www.konradborkowski.com). On the isle of Rum, I was greatly assisted by Linda Hjoelund of Scottish National Heritage and all the staff at Kinloch Castle, especially Georgie McMillan and Rebecca Watson. Thanks also to Dave 'Chainsaw' Beaton for loaning me his binoculars. On Canna, a big thank you to Stewart Connor, the island's National Trust for Scotland warden and his partner, Julie McCabe, who rescued us when our tent was blown into the sea. Special thanks are due to my wife, The Lovely Fiona, for her support, encouragement and great good sense.

Wild goats at Harris Bay, Ruinsival in the background (Walk 3, Day 2)

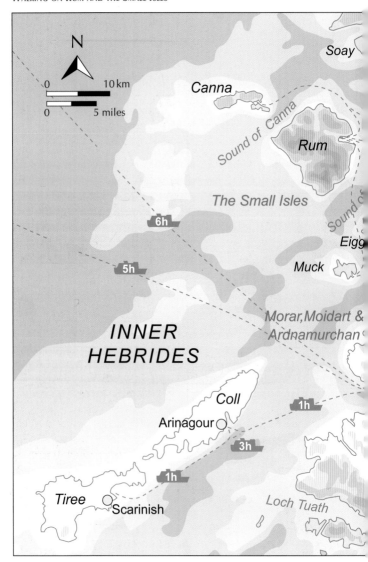

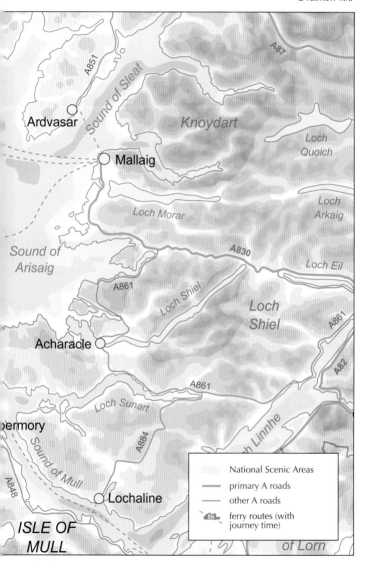

9

Climbing to the Bealach Bairc-mheall, from Coire Dubh (Walk 1)

INTRODUCTION

Askival, with Ainshval beyond from the summit of Hallival (Walk 1)

The wild, beautiful and remote Small Isles lie scattered off Scotland's Atlantic coast, north of Ardnamurchan, west of Morar, south of Skye and east of the Outer Hebridean isles of Barra and South Uist. To the south-west, the Small Isles' near neighbours, Coll and Tiree – the Hebridean Twins, lie to the west of Mull. The Small Isles, Coll and Tiree provide the adventurous walker with a fine and diverse range of walking, from the towering peaks of the Rum Cuillin to the dunes and machair pastures of low-lying Tiree.

Many of the routes in this guidebook are coastal walks traversing extremely varied terrain, from rugged, rocky shores and vertiginous cliffs to vast expanses of flower-carpeted machair and white sandy beaches.

These coastal landscapes teem with wildlife, and with remarkable geological features, including raised beaches, caves, natural arches, sea stacks and basalt dikes. Many traces of the islands' histories, both ancient and more recent, are found around these coastlines, from Bronze Age duns (fortifications) perched on rocky promontories to abandoned settlements, mute testaments to the Highland Clearances.

The Small Isles are often referred to as the 'hidden gems' of the Western Isles – and with good cause. Although blessed with great natural beauty, the islands tend to be overlooked, literally and metaphorically, by the many visitors drawn to the famously scenic grandeur of

Natural arch north-east of Guirdil Bay (Walk 3, Day 2)

Skye, their renowned and imposing neighbour.

The relative dearth of visitors is partly due to the Small Isles having few roads or metalled tracks and visitors only being allowed to bring vehicles by special arrangement. Furthermore, although the islands' amenities are generally excellent, they are far from extensive. Therefore, planning a walking trip to the Small Isles requires a degree of logistical forethought – just getting here can be an undertaking in itself.

The upside is the real sense of remoteness that is found among the hills, along the rugged coastlines and beach-garlanded shores of these wonderful islands; they are a haven for those who like to get away from the madding crowd and enjoy the peace and freedom of walking through landscapes unaffected by large-scale tourism.

The Small Isles are appositely named; Rum, the largest of the group, is just 14km (8½ miles) north to south by 13.5km (8½ miles) east to west. Yet this relatively small area offers remarkable scope for the adventurous and experienced walker. Given the relative size of the island and the range of excellent walking available, Rum is the main focus of this guidebook, with extensive sections on the fascinating geology, history and wildlife of the island.

WHEN TO GO

In late spring, summer and early autumn you are more likely to benefit from mild weather. May and June tend to be the finest months, although rain – often torrential – can be a feature at any time of year. During the milder months the highly aggressive island midge abounds in alarming numbers on Rum and Eigg, less so on the breezier islands. Deer ticks are also most active in warmer weather. If properly protected against rain, midges and ticks (see What to take), late spring through to autumn provides the longest days, useful if you're attempting a round of the Rum Cuillin or when staying at remote bothies. Obviously there are more visitors at these times of year; you're more likely to encounter other walkers, and the bothies and bays are also visited by intrepid sea-kayakers.

In winter you're almost guaranteed to have the islands' hinterlands to yourself, but you'll have very short days and wild weather is a strong possibility. But it can be surprisingly mild in winter, thanks to the benign influence of the Gulf Stream, and if you're lucky you might enjoy some crystal-clear, sunlit winter days. The terrain can be very boggy in winter, with December and January being the wettest months on the islands. Crossing burns and rivers can be hazardous when they are in spate after heavy rain. Before setting out to walk in winter, ensure you are properly equipped and let others know your planned route.

GETTING TO THE FERRY

Travellers to Scotland's west coast usually come via Glasgow. Trains from the south come into Glasgow

Rain over Canna seen from Guirdil bothy, Rum (Walk TBC)

Central. Trains for Mallaig, Oban and the islands leave from Glasgow Queen Street, a ten minute walk from Glasgow Central. (You can catch a shuttle bus or taxi between the stations. To get from one to the other on foot, leave Central via the main entrance into Gordon Street, turn right (east) along Gordon Street, continue across Union Street and Mitchell Street into Buchanan Street. Turn left (north) and continue until you reach St Vincent Place. Cross St Vincent Place here, turn right and follow the left-hand (north) side of St Vincent Place till you reach George Square. Turn left and continue to the crossing on West George Street. Cross West George Street and continue up a slight slope and then steps into the Queen Street station concourse.)

The Small Isles are usually accessed from Mallaig. Coll and Tiree are reached by ferry from Oban.

Glasgow to Mallaig

By train

The direct service between Glasgow Queen Street and Mallaig takes 5hrs 20mins. The train connects with the Saturday afternoon sailing in summer. Take the train the previous evening to connect with the early ferries. Alternatively, it is possible to take the train from Fort William to Mallaig to connect with some ferry crossings on the morning of departure. See www.scotrail.co.uk for timetable information.

By road

Take the A82 from Glasgow (or the Erskine Bridge, if bypassing Glasgow on the M8) towards Loch Lomond and the Trossachs National Park. Keep to the A82 until Fort William. From Fort William, continue west along the A830 to Mallaig. The drive takes around 3½–4hrs. Long stay parking is available free of charge around the bay in Mallaig.

By bus

Scottish Citylink operates a coach service between Glasgow and Mallaig, changing at Fort William, taking around 5hrs. Travel to Mallaig the evening before to make the early morning ferry. Alternatively, it is possible to take the coach from Fort William to Mallaig to connect with the ferry on the morning of departure. Consult the relevant timetables at www.citylink.co.uk or contact the travel centre at Buchanan Street Bus Station on 0141 332 7133.

Glasgow to Oban

By train

The direct train service between Glasgow Queen Street and Oban takes around 3hrs 5mins. Except for the Tuesday service in summer, it is necessary to take the train to Oban the previous evening to make the early ferry departure. See www.scotrail.co.uk for timetable information.

Boarding the MV Lochnevis, Canna

By road
Take the A82 from Glasgow (or the Erskine Bridge, if bypassing Glasgow on the M8) towards Loch Lomond and the Trossachs National Park. Keep to the A82 until Tyndrum. At Tyndrum head west along the A85, passing through Dalmally then along the north shore of Loch Awe, through Taynuilt and along the south shore of Loch Etive before arriving at Oban in around 2½–3hrs.

By bus
Scottish Citylink Coaches operates an extensive bus service between Glasgow and Oban that takes around 3hrs. Except for the Tuesday service in summer, it is necessary to take the coach to Oban the previous evening to make the early morning ferry departure. Consult the relevant timetables at www.citylink.co.uk or contact the Travel Centre at Buchanan Street Bus Station on 0141 332 7133.

Caledonian MacBrayne operates the principal ferry service from Mallaig to Rum and the Small Isles every day except Sunday, year round.

Rum
In summer there is one crossing a day Monday–Thursday, with two crossings on Friday and Saturday; in winter, one crossing a day. The crossing takes 1hr 15mins direct, 3hrs 40mins via Eigg and Muck and 3hrs 20mins via Canna.

Eigg
In summer there is one crossing a day to Eigg Monday–Friday (no sailing on Wednesdays) with two crossings on Saturdays. In winter there is one crossing a day with no crossings on Tuesdays and Thursdays. The crossing takes 1hr 20mins direct and up to 5hrs via Canna, Rum and Muck.

Muck

In summer there is one crossing a day to Muck on Tuesdays, Thursdays and Fridays and two crossings on Saturdays. In winter there is one crossing a day on Mondays, Wednesdays, Fridays and Saturdays. The crossing takes 2hrs via Eigg and 4hrs 50mins via Canna and Rum.

Canna

In summer there is one crossing a day to Canna on Mondays, Wednesdays and Fridays, and two crossings on Saturdays. In winter there is one crossing a day on Tuesdays, Thursdays and Saturdays only. The crossing takes 2hrs 5mins direct and 3hrs 55mins via Eigg and Rum.

There are various crossings between the islands on the outward and inward sailings from and to Mallaig. Visit www.calmac.co.uk for timetable details or call the port office

in Mallaig on 01687 462403. Bicycles are carried free of charge. Cars are only permitted for residents.

A ferry service is also run by Arisaig Marine, which operates the MV Sheerwater between Arisaig and the Small Isles during the summer months. For details visit www.arisaig.co.uk or call 01687 450224.

AquaXplore operate a fast RIB (rigid inflatable boat) service from Elgol on Skye to Rum and Canna. Advance booking recommended. Tel 01471 866244.

Coll and Tiree

Caledonian MacBrayne operates the car ferry service between Oban, Arinagour (Coll) and Scarinish (Tiree). There is one crossing each day in summer, Monday–Sunday, with an extra service from Barra in the Outer Hebrides on Thursdays. In winter the service is reduced to

The dramatic cliff top of Am Beannan on Canna with north-west Rum beyond (Walk 10)

Heading north-east along the coast of Rum, Bloodstone Hill in the background (Walk 3, Day 3)

one crossing a day on Tuesdays, Thursdays, Saturdays and Sundays only. You can also take the ferry between Coll and Tiree, which is a journey of around an hour.

The crossing from Oban to Coll takes between 2½hrs and 3hrs (depending on the vessel).

The crossing from Oban to Tiree goes via Coll and takes between 3½hrs and 4hrs (depending on the vessel).

Check the Caledonian MacBrayne website – www.calmac.co.uk – for timetables or call the port office at Oban on 01631 566688.

Flybe fly to and from Tiree from Glasgow Airport every day except Sunday; flights take approximately 50mins: www.flybe.com. Hebridean Airways fly to and from Tiree from Connel Airport near Oban on Monday, Wednesday and some

Fridays. Flights take 35mins direct or 1hr via Colonsay: www.hebrideanair. co.uk, or Tel 01236 780120.

MAPS, ROUTE FINDING AND ACCESS

This guidebook includes detailed descriptions of 16 coastal and hill routes on these often rugged and sublimely beautiful islands. Some of the walks included here have not appeared in any previous guide: none of them with the Ordnance Survey route maps and detailed route descriptions in this guidebook. These are mostly demanding routes in terms of the terrain, length of route or both. The terrain covered is extremely varied, often challenging and mostly without waymarks or established footpaths. But the

Climbing above the cliff tops at Sgorr Reidh (Walk 3, Day 2)

rewards are plentiful, as these routes traverse some breathtakingly beautiful scenery alive with a profusion of plants and wildlife and full of historical interest.

Maps

It is essential that you have the appropriate maps for the walks described in this guidebook. There are few waymarks, signposts or paths of any kind, making accurate route finding all the more important. A degree of navigational proficiency is indispensable.

This guide incorporates Ordnance Survey 1:50,000 mapping with highlighted routes. These should be used in conjunction with OS Explorer 1:25,000 maps because of their greater topographic detail. Do not rely solely on the maps in this guidebook as it is essential that you are able to ascertain your position in the wider context, should you need

to abandon your walk and make for the nearest road or habitation. The walks described in this guidebook are covered by the following Ordnance Survey maps:

- OS Explorer 1:25,000 sheet 397 *Rum, Eigg, Muck, Canna and Sanday*
- OS Explorer 1:25,000 sheet 372 *Coll and Tiree*
- OS Landranger 1:50,000 sheet 39 *Rum, Eigg, Muck and Canna*
- OS Landranger 1:50,000 sheet 46 *Coll and Tiree*

A compass is indispensable and a 'wristwatch' altimeter is also very useful for navigation, especially on the hills of Rum. It's not quite so easy to get lost when walking along the island coastlines, but it is important that you know exactly where you are, especially in poor weather or visibility and if for any reason you need to head inland from the coast.

Access

The Land Reform (Scotland) Act 2003 established legal right of non-motorised public access over most land and inland water in Scotland. The Act is supported by the Scottish Outdoor Access Code. In effect, the Act means that walkers have the right to roam, but should exercise that right in ways which are compatible with land management needs. Forestry, deerstalking, grouse shooting, lambing and other farming and crofting practices are the activities most liable to restrict walkers' movements. This is as much the case in the Hebrides as in the Highlands.

Except around Kinloch on Rum there is precious little forestry in the Small Isles, Coll and Tiree. Rum is also the only island with a deer population and, consequently, deerstalking. The stalking season runs from mid-August to mid-February: if you plan to walk on the island during this period it is advisable to contact the Head Stalker, Derek Thomson, on 01687 462030 or 07768 249833. Between March and May it is important to avoid disturbing sheep during lambing. Avoiding interference with other farming and crofting practices is usually accomplished with minimal inconvenience.

Wild camping is permitted but please check the Outdoor Access Code for information about your rights and responsibilities (www.outdooraccess-scotland.com). For more on camping on Rum see Appendix B.

SAFETY AND EMERGENCIES

In fine weather the Inner Hebrides can seem like an earthly paradise; however the onset of high winds and driving rain can rapidly make the place feel quite hellish, especially if you are exposed to the elements. It is essential that you are properly equipped and are

Looking down to Harris Bay from the summit of Barkeval (Walk 1)

able to navigate proficiently in poor visibility. Check the weather forecast before setting out and allow yourself plenty of time to complete your day's itinerary during daylight. Always let someone know your intended route and estimated time of completion.

Carry a first aid kit, survival blanket, mobile phone and plenty of food. Wear at least one item of high-visibility clothing. A whistle and/or torch are important for attracting attention in case of injury. Six blasts on the whistle or six torch flashes should be repeated every minute. In case of injury or other incident, try to stay calm and assess your situation. If anyone is injured remember ABC – airway, breathing, circulation (signs of life, blood loss). Make any casualties warm and comfortable and place any unconscious casualties in the recovery position.

Try to ascertain your exact position on the map and consider your options for walking to safety, finding shelter, staying put or seeking help. (Remember that it may take an emergency team some hours to reach you, especially in poor conditions in a remote area.) If you decide to call for help, phone 999 and ask for the Police and Mountain Rescue. Be ready to give the location of the incident (grid references, map sheet number, name of the area and description of the terrain), number and names of people in the party and their condition, any injuries and names of casualties. Be prepared to supply the numbers of any phones carried by the party, and describe the nature and time of the incident, weather conditions including wind speed and visibility at the incident site, equipment at the site, including warm clothing and shelter, distinguishing features and markers at the site, and the location from which you are phoning if different from the incident site.

Some of the walks described here are challenging and best not attempted on your own. Likewise, these routes should only be undertaken by fit and experienced walkers and are not

Heading east along the Kinloch Glen track (Walk 7)

Campfire at Harris Bay (Walk 3 Day 2, Walk 7)

suitable for the very elderly, very young or anyone carrying an injury. Only fit, properly equipped, experienced hill-walkers with good navigation skills should attempt a round of the Rum Cuillin – and then only in good conditions. The weather can change very rapidly in this maritime mountain environment. The terrain is difficult in places and visibility can be lost with little warning.

After heavy rain or snowfall many burns and rivers run very high, with a terrific volume of fast-moving water. This is especially the case on mountainous Rum. Do not attempt to cross rivers in spate – if you are swept away your chances of survival are very small. If you're successful in crossing one river in such conditions you may come up against an impassable torrent further on; if you then attempt to recross the river you previously crossed, you may find that it is running higher and faster than before.

WHAT TO TAKE

OS Explorer 1:25,000 maps are indispensable (a waterproof map case is advisable), as is a compass. A 'wristwatch' altimeter is also very useful. A robust rucksack with adequate capacity and a comfortable harness is indispensable, as is a waterproof pack liner. For day walks, a 30+ litre pack should be sufficient; for longer trips, when you are carrying camping gear and several days' food, a 60+ litre pack may be required. Effective waterproofs are essential when undertaking a walk of any length in the Hebrides. Weather can change quickly on the islands and doesn't always obey the forecasts.

Lightweight, 'wickable', quick-drying clothing is a must when walking the often strenuous routes in this guide. Carry adequate warm clothing: extra layers are useful when you take breaks. The nature of much of the terrain – on Rum, Eigg and Canna especially – requires robust walking boots with ankle support and a Vibram sole. On Coll, Tiree and Muck, you may find that good quality Vibram-soled walking 'trainers' are sufficient. It is difficult to keep your feet dry at the best of times when walking on the islands, so Gore-Tex-lined or well-waxed boots are essential.

Gaiters are indispensable on terrain that can be very boggy in places. Telescopic walking poles are very useful, especially when carrying a heavy pack on multi-day walks. A warm hat and gloves should find a place in your rucksack, even in summer. Sun cream, a sun hat and sunglasses should also be carried from spring through to autumn. Always carry plenty of food, including high-energy snacks, and plenty of water. With the exceptions of Tiree and Muck, there are frequent opportunities to fill up from the islands' many burns. The water is generally safe to drink; however, take water-purifying tablets if you are worried about contamination.

A basic medical kit and a survival bag should always be carried and a mobile phone is useful in case of misadventure. A head torch is invaluable if you are benighted and can help to attract attention in an emergency; carrying a whistle is useful for the same

purpose. From late spring until late autumn it is worth carrying some serious insect repellent (some swear by Avon 'Skin So Soft') and a midge/mosquito hat – or net to place over a hat – are useful lines of defence against *Culicoides impunctatus*. The O'Tom tick removing fork is the best tool for this delicate job. Lightweight binoculars are worth their weight for admiring the islands' splendid wildlife.

USING THIS GUIDE

The routes are grouped by island into six sections, each preceded by an overview map. Each section has an introduction covering the local geology, history, wildlife, transport and amenities, including information on the local access situation and estate contacts.

Route descriptions

Each route in this guide is described step by step and is illustrated with extracts from the 1:50,000 OS maps. For each one the route distance, rough timing and the OS map you will need to carry with you are listed, alongside the grid reference for your start point. Altitudes are given in metres, abbreviated to m, for example '750m'. Distances along the ground are given in metres, fully spelled out, for example '100 metres'.

In the appendices at the end of the book are a route summary table, details of accommodation island by island, and suggestions for further reading.

RUM
Rùm

Heading east to Glen Shellesder with Bloodstone Hill towering above Glen Guirdil to the west (Walk 3, Day 3)

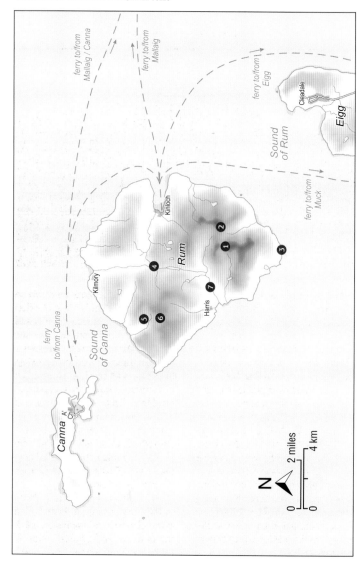

INTRODUCTION

On the Dibidil pony path, with Sgurr nan Gillean dominating the horizon (Walk 3, Day 1)

Rum is by far the largest of the Small Isles, and at some 100 square kilometres and 14km (8½ miles) north to south by 13.5km (8½ miles) east to west is the 15th largest of the Scottish islands. It is the wettest and arguably the most mountainous island of its size in Britain. Its striking profile of jagged basalt and gabbro mountain peaks testifies to its volcanic origins. Rum's highest peaks, Askival (812m) and Ainshval (781m), are Corbetts – those Scottish mountains between 2500 and 3000 feet (762m and 914m) with a relative height of at least 500ft (152m): Rum is the smallest Scottish island to have a summit over 762m (2500ft).

Kinloch, the island's only settlement, is at the head of Loch Scresort, the main anchorage, some 27km west of Mallaig and the Morar peninsula on the mainland. Rum is 11km (7 miles) south of Skye at its nearest point and 23km (14 miles) north-west of the Ardnamurchan peninsula. Rum has a tiny population – around 30 – and when the village of Kinloch is left behind a true sense of remoteness is soon found amid the island's wild, dramatic and sometimes challenging landscape. The only other habitations, besides the bothies at Dibidil and Guirdil, are the red deer research base at Kilmory Bay and the Scottish National Heritage (SNH) lodge at Harris.

The distinctive volcanic chain of hills comprising the Rum Cuillin is the obvious and immediate draw for outdoor enthusiasts, whether for hill walking, scrambling or rock

Rum ponies at Harris (Walk 3, Day 2 and Walk 7)

climbing. A round of the Rum Cuillin makes for a challenging day in the hills and usually features somewhere on the 'to-do' list of Scottish mountain aficionados.

But for the adventurous walker there is much more to Rum than the Cuillin. This guidebook includes detailed route descriptions for five major walks – including a three-day walk around the coast and circular routes around the remote western hills – and several shorter routes.

Land Rover tracks cross the island from Kinloch to Kilmory and Harris, and there are several long-established footpaths, including the well worn track up the Allt Slugan to the Coire Dubh – gateway to the Rum Cuillin – and the pony path around the coast from Kinloch to Dibidil bothy and Papadil. Other areas lack distinct paths, necessitating detailed route descriptions and mapping – all

the more so as Rum is exceptionally prone to cloud cover, with associated implications for navigation. Walking conditions on Rum are often wet and rough: it is essential that walkers are properly prepared and equipped.

Staying on Rum

Rum's community is undergoing a period of change with the phased transfer of assets from Scottish Natural Heritage to the Isle of Rum Community Trust. The Trust now owns around 35 hectares of land and 11 residential properties in and around Kinloch, and is tasked with managing community land and assets for the community and the visiting public, alongside promoting sustainable rural regeneration.

As a result the accommodation situation is in a period of flux, and it is worth checking the Isle of Rum website well in advance of a visit to see what is available: www.isleofrum.com. Accommodation provision at the time of writing can be found in Appendix B.

GEOLOGY

The Rum Cuillin forms the impressive skyline of jagged peaks dominating the south of the island.

The northern peaks of the range are principally formed of peridotite basalt and gabbro, similar in construction to the Black Cuillin of Skye.

The southern peaks are Torridonian sandstone capped with quartz-felsite and Lewisian gneiss, and the rounded granite hills of Ard Nev, Orval, Sròn an t-Saighdeir, Fionchra and the lava-capped summit of Bloodstone Hill are in the island's west.

Rum is the core of a volcano that developed on a pre-existing structure of Torridonian sandstone and shales resting on Lewisian Gneiss. Volcanic activity 65 million years ago formed a dome over a kilometre high and several kilometres across. Pressure from below caused fractures to form around the dome, which collapsed, forming a caldera. The caldera floor was gradually covered by rocks and debris, consisting largely of Torridonian sandstone and Lewisian gneiss, which was compressed, forming rocks known as breccias, found in Coire Dubh. The vestiges of the dome are evident on the slopes of the Rum Cuillin, where

Looking from Askival to Trollaval (right) and Ainshval (left), with Ruinsival beyond (Walk 1) (photo: Peter Khambatta)

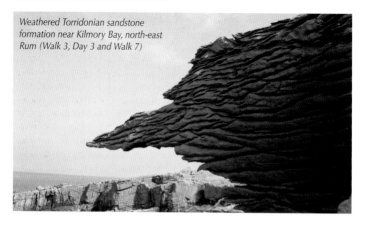

Weathered Torridonian sandstone formation near Kilmory Bay, north-east Rum (Walk 3, Day 3 and Walk 7)

the Torridonian rocks incline steeply away from the adjacent igneous rocks.

Magma, ash and rock erupted into the caldera, along with gas clouds known as pyroclastic flows which formed rocks known as rhyodacites, found around the margins of the Rum Cuillin and on the ridge between the summits of Ainshval and Sgùrr nan Gillean.

The western hills, including Orval and Ard Nev, are predominantly composed of coarse-grained granites formed from magma that crystallised below the Earth's surface. The Rum Cuillin is mostly composed of layers of pale, hard gabbro interspersed with brown, crumbly peridotite, rocks created from cooling magma at the base of the magma chamber, especially on Hallival and Askival. There are some outcrops of the pre-volcanic Lewisian gneiss near Dibidil in the south-east corner of the island, and extensive

Torridonian sandstone is found in the north and east.

Basalt dikes are found on the north-west coast between Kilmory and Guirdil: erosion of the less-resistant rock into which they are intruded has left them exposed as natural walls. They tend to radiate out from a point in Glen Harris, which suggests that this was the centre of volcanic activity. Bloodstone Hill was formed by lava flowing away from this volcanic centre; gas bubbles in the rock filled with heated silica, which cooled to form green agate flecked with red, hence the name 'bloodstone'.

The last major glaciation of the Quarternary Ice Age began about 30,000 years ago, when glaciers covered the island and the tops of the highest mountains protruded through the ice as 'nunataks'. Frost-shattering created scree slopes on these summits, and freeze-thaw processes have sorted rock particles into remarkable regular patterns such as the stone stripes and polygons near the summit of Orval.

The ice sheets retreated around 10,000BC. During glacial periods sea levels dropped, rising again when the glaciers melted. The landmass sank under the weight of the ice cap, then rose again as the ice retreated. The land continued to rise beyond the maximum increase in sea level, forming the raised beaches found around the coastline 12–30m above the present sea level, especially between Harris and A'Bhrideanach.

Tundra vegetation gave way to forest. The climate warmed 6000 years ago, encouraging forestation to a higher altitude than at present, before becoming cooler and damper around 1000BC, and peat expanded at the expense of woodland. A dearth of cultivable land also led to woodland clearance by early farming communities.

HISTORY
Mankind probably first reached parts of Scotland during the mild phases of the last glacial periods of the Quarternary Ice Age, but retreated as the climate deteriorated. All traces of Palaeolithic (Old Stone Age) settlement were obliterated by the ice sheets during the subsequent glaciation. Archaeological evidence established the existence of Mesolithic (Middle Stone Age) settlement in some areas of Scotland from around 6500BC, with hunter-gatherers

in seasonal occupation as early as 10,500BC on the fringes of the retreating ice sheet.

Traces of the earliest known human settlement in Scotland were found on Rum at a site near Kinloch. Concentrations of bloodstone microliths indicated the manufacture of stone tools and roasted hazlenut shells were radiocarbon dated to 6500BC. A shell midden at Papadil, cave middens at Bagh na h-Uamha and Shellesder and tidal fish traps at Kinloch and Kilmory are also characteristic of Mesolithic hunter-gatherers.

The Stone Age to St Columba
Peat core samples from Kinloch revealed soil erosion and a decline in tree pollen, suggesting that woodland clearance for cultivation occured during the Neolithic (New Stone Age), from around 2700BC. Bronze Age traces on Rum are limited to hut circle sites and finds of barbed and tanged bloodstone arrow heads. Like many marginal Bronze Age settlements, Rum may have been abandoned during a period of harsh climatic conditions prevailing in northern Europe after the eruption of the Icelandic volcano, Hekla, about 1150.

Iron-working skills and characteristic structures including brochs, duns, wheelhouses, crannogs and souterrains were introduced to Scotland around the middle of the first millenium BC by Celtic people migrating from continental Europe. Rum possesses only a few crude promontory fort sites at Kilmory, Papadil and Shellesder. Decorated pottery sherds are the only other Iron Age artefacts retrieved on the island.

The first written references to the early Caledonian people come from the Romans, following Agricola's expedition north in AD81. References to the 'Picti' first appeared in Roman accounts around AD300, but it is probable that the Picts were an assortment of racial and cultural groups – including the aboriginal Bronze Age peoples – bound together by the threat of the Romans. It is likely that the population of Rum at this time was Pictish in origin.

Early in the third century an Irish tribe – Scotti of Dál Riata – began the colonisation of Kintyre and the Inner Hebrides. The process of conquering and colonisation continued until late in the fifth century when the kingdom of Dalriada established its capital at Dunadd, following the decisive invasion of Argyll. St Columba came from Ireland to Iona around 563 and established a monastery that became an important centre of learning and spirituality. Columba's followers, the early Celtic Christian missionaries, set about converting the populations of the islands and the mainland. One of their number, Beccan the Solitary, became a monk at Iona in 623 and then a hermit – probably on Rum.

The Viking era
In 794 Iona suffered the first of many Viking raids, which gradually forced the monastery into decline. In common with many Hebridean islands, Rum came within the Norse sphere of influence. The Norsemen ruled the Small Isles from 833 until the Treaty of Perth in 1266, when the Isle of Man and all the Hebrides were ceded to Scotland. The only tangible evidence of a Norse presence on Rum to date is a piece of carved narwhal ivory unearthed at Bagh na h-Uamh in 1940.

The Norse legacy is most obvious in the toponymy of the island, whose name may itself derive from the Old Norse *rōm-øy*, meaning 'wide island', or the Gaelic *ì-dhruim*, meaning 'isle of the ridge'. The name 'cuillin' also comes from the Norse *kiolen*, meaning 'high rocks'. Several of the principal peaks have Norse names, with '-val' deriving from *fjall*, meaning 'hill': Askival (812m) and Ainshval (781m) ('spear-shaped hill' and 'rocky ridge hill' respectively), Hallival (722m), Trollaval ('mountain of the trolls', 700m), Barkeval ('precipice hill', 591m), Ruinsival ('stone-heap hill', 528m): Gaelic names are Sgùrr nan Goibhrean ('goat hill', 759m) and Sgùrr nan Gillean ('peak of the young men', 764m). The place-names Dibidil and Papadil are Norse.

The Middle Ages to the Macleans
During the 13th century the island was in the possession of the powerful Macruari clan for a brief period until 1346, when Rum was chartered to Clanranald – known as the Lords

of the Isles – who ruled much of the Hebrides from Finlaggan on Islay for 150 years. The Lordship came to an end after John MacDonald II's duplicitous treaty with Edward IV of England against the Scottish Crown, which led to the forfeiture of all MacDonald land.

From the early Medieval period Rum was noted for its deer and 'excellent sport' and was probably used as a hunting reserve by the nobility. By the mid-16th century Rum was in the possession of the MacLeans of Coll, then in 1588 the Small Isles were assaulted when Lachlan Maclean of Duart led a raiding party including 100 Spanish marines from a galleon of the defeated Armada anchored at Tobermory. The islands' settlements were torched and their inhabitants murdered. In 1593 King James VI received a report indicating that Clanranald had re-occupied the island, but despite these temporary setbacks the Macleans of Coll kept possession of Rum for more than three centuries.

By the late 17th century Rum's status as a hunting reserve had declined and the human population had increased. The inhabitants caught fish, grew barley and potatoes and raised Black cattle for export to the mainland. Conditions were primitive and the dearth of viable farming land stretched resources. The needs of a growing population led to the extermination of the native red

Kinloch Castle

31

deer during the latter half of the 18th century.

At the beginning of the 19th century there were nine hamlets on Rum and the local economy enjoyed a boost from the kelp industry. However, in 1825 the island was leased to Dr Lachlan Maclean, a relative of Hugh Maclean of Coll. Like many Highland landlords, Maclean, in search of profit, decided to clear the land and turn it over to 8000 blackface sheep. Rum's population was given a year's notice to quit its homes. On 11 July 1826 around 300 inhabitants boarded the Highland Lad and the Dove of Harmony, bound for Cape Breton in Nova Scotia. The remaining 130 followed in 1828 on the St. Lawrence, along with some 150 inhabitants of Muck, another of Maclean of Coll's properties. Then mutton and wool prices declined and the enterprise failed; Lachlan Maclean left Rum, bankrupt, in 1839.

Into the 20th century

In 1845 MacLean of Coll sold Rum to the Marquess of Salisbury, who reintroduced red deer and converted the island into a sporting estate, and for over a century Rum was known as the 'Forbidden Island', as uninvited visitors were actively discouraged.

After the Marquess of Salisbury's death, the island was bought by Farquhar Campbell in 1870, who passed it on to his nephew. In 1888 Rum was acquired by John Bullough, a cotton machinery manufacturer and

self-made millionaire from Accrington in Lancashire who had previously leased the island's shooting rights. The prospectus for the 1888 sale described Rum as: 'The most picturesque of the islands which lie off the west coast of Scotland, it is altogether a property of exceptional attractions...as a sporting estate it has at present few equals'. At this time the population numbered between 60 and 70 shepherds, estate workers and their families. When Bullough died in 1891, ownership of the island was assumed by his son, George Bullough.

Sir George Bullough – he was knighted in 1901 – changed the traditional spelling of the island's name to Rhum in 1905, allegedly to avoid the connotations in the title Laird of Rum (the spelling reverted to Rum in 1992 when SNH took over from the NCC). However, Sir George's most striking legacy is the incongruous and often maligned Kinloch Castle, built during the last years of the 19th century and completed in 1902. The castle was built from red sandstone quarried at Annan in Dumfriesshire. A hundred stonemasons and craftsmen were brought from Lancashire, and Sir George purportedly paid the workforce extra to wear kilts of Rum plaid.

The estate employed around a hundred people, including 14 under-gardeners to maintain the extensive grounds, which included a nine-hole golf course, a bowling green, tennis and racquets courts, heated ornamental turtle and alligator ponds and an

Sir George Bullough's collection of exotic Edwardiana adorns the interior of Kinloch castle

aviary housing birds of paradise and humming birds. Soil for the grounds was imported from Ayrshire, and grapes, peaches, nectarines and figs were grown in the estate's glasshouses. The interior boasted an orchestrion – a mechanical contrivance that could simulate the sounds of brass, drum and woodwind – an air-conditioned billiards room and an ingenious and elaborate central heating system, which fed piping hot water to the Heath Robinson-esque bathrooms, replete with 'jacuzzi', while also heating the glasshouses and ornamental ponds.

Sir George and Lady Monica Bullough usually resided at Kinloch Castle during the stalking season and would entertain their wealthy and important guests in some style. Deer stalking was one of the primary diversions for the Bulloughs and their guests and a day's stalking on the hill would be followed by a sumptuous evening meal served at the dining suite, which had originally graced the state rooms of Sir George's yacht Rhouma. After dinner the company would repair to the magnificent ballroom, with its highly polished sprung floors and cut glass chandelier, to dance the night away.

This exalted era drew to a close with the coming of the Great War. Most of the estate's male staff went to Flanders and many never came back. The estate fell into disrepair during the war and as Britain's fortunes

Harris Bay and the Bullough mausoleum (Walk 3, Day 2 and Walk 7)

declined in the post-war years, the Bullough finances also gradually dwindled, along with their interest in Rum. Sir George died in France in July 1939 and was interred in the family Mausoleum at Harris Bay. His widow continued to visit Rum as late as 1954. She died in 1967, aged 98, and was buried next to her husband in the Mausoleum at Harris, having sold the whole island, save for the Mausoleum, but including the castle and its contents, to the NCC in 1957 for the 'knock-down price of £23,000' on the understanding that it would be used as a National Nature Reserve.

The NNR

In 2010, SNH handed over Kinloch Village to the Isle of Rum Community Trust to provide land for housing and local enterprises. The island still is owned and managed as a single estate

by the NCC's successors, Scottish Natural Heritage (SNH). In addition to its status as a NNR, Rum was designated a Biosphere Reserve in 1976, a Site of Special Scientific Interest in 1987, and has 17 sites scheduled as nationally important ancient monuments.

The Rum NNR was originally envisaged as an 'open-air laboratory' with scientific research conducted into specific areas of the island's ecology, most notably the long term study of the red deer population. Rum was also the primary site for the ultimately successful reintroduction of the white-tailed eagle to Scotland during the 1970s and 1980s. However, SNH has shifted the emphasis to re-creating a habitat resembling what existed before the island's native tree cover was removed. This has involved the reintroduction of over a million trees and shrubs of 20 native species in the vicinity of Kinloch and Loch Scresort.

Magnus Magnusson's well-regarded book on Rum is entitled *Nature's Island* – an apposite description of this mountainous island wilderness, where it is easy to imagine a past without much human presence. However you can also revisit the isle's more decadent human past at Kinloch Castle.

WILDLIFE

Rum's red deer population has been the subject of a long term study by researchers from Cambridge and Edinburgh universities, based at Kilmory Bay in the north of the island. The research has focussed on the sociobiology and behavioural ecology of red deer. The island's deer population was hunted to extinction in the 18th century, but since reintroduction in 1845 the number has grown to the currently maintained level of around 1500.

The island has a small herd of about 14 ponies. The Rum Ponies are an old breed, and their presence was first recorded in 1772. Shortly thereafter, Dr Johnson described them as 'very small, but of a breed eminent for beauty'. They are of stocky stature, averaging 13 hands height, with a dark stripe along the back and zebra stripes on the forelegs. These features suggest that they are related to primitive northern European breeds, perhaps introduced by the Norsemen. It is sometimes claimed – erroneously – that they are descended from animals off-loaded from ships of the Spanish Armada. The ponies are used to bring

During the autumn rut the night air on Rum resounds with the 'belling' roar of stags (photo: Konrad Borkowski)

Red deer near Guirdil bothy

deer carcasses off the hill during the stalking season, but are otherwise left to roam wild.

Rum's wild goats are subject to the same Armada myth as the ponies, but are in fact descended from domestic animals. The goat stocks were improved for stalking during the Bullough's tenure and were renowned for their impressive horns and thick, shaggy fleeces. The tribe, numbering around 200, usually inhabits the sea cliffs and mountains, particularly in the west. A small herd of around 30 Highland cattle was introduced to the island in 1970.

Atlantic grey and common seals frequent Rum's coastline, and Eurasian otters patrol territories around the island's shores. Other mammals found on Rum include the pygmy shrew, pipistrelle bat, brown rat and the island's own strain of long-tailed field mouse, *Apodemus sylvaticus hamiltoni*. The only reptile found on Rum is the common lizard, and the only amphibian is the palmate newt. There are brown trout, European eels and three-spined sticklebacks in the streams, and occasionally salmon in the Kinloch River.

Rum is renowned for its 61,000 pairs of Manx shearwaters – one of the world's largest breeding colonies. These migratory birds return to Rum every summer to breed in underground burrows high in the Cuillin. Trollaval has high densities of nest burrows, which may have been occupied for many centuries. When the birds swap incubation shifts at night they make a fearsome racket, hence the Norse name for the mountain. There are sizeable colonies of fulmars, shags, guillemots, razorbills, kittiwakes and other gulls, mainly found along the south-eastern cliffs.

White-tailed eagles were persecuted to extinction on Rum by 1912 and became extinct in Scotland thereafter. A programme of reintroduction began on the island in 1975, and within ten years 82 young birds from Norway had been released. Today a successful breeding population is gradually colonising the west coast of Scotland. Several pairs of golden eagles nest on the island; merlin, buzzards, sparrowhawks, peregrines, kestrels and short-eared owls are the other resident birds of prey. Other bird species include the red-throated diver, red-breasted merganser, eider, shelduck, red grouse, corncrake, oystercatcher, lapwing, golden plover, curlew, cuckoo, raven and hooded crow as well as various finches, tits, chats, thrushes, warblers, pipits and wagtails.

Invertebrates include numerous species of damselfly, dragonfly, beetles, butterflies and moths. Several rare species are found on the slopes of Barkeval, Hallival and Askival including the ground beetles *Leistus montanus* and *Amara quenseli*. The hugely irritating midge (*Culicoides impunctatus*), a small biting gnat, occurs in unbelievable numbers between midspring and mid-autumn. Deer ticks and clegs – an aggressive horse fly

– are the island's other bloodthirsty beasties. Ticks can carry Lyme disease, which can become seriously debilitating if undiagnosed and untreated.

WOODLAND, PLANTS AND FLOWERS

By the end of the 18th century much of Rum's woodland had been cleared for grazing. John Bullough planted 8000 trees at Kilmory, Harris and Kinloch in the 1890s, but only some of those at Kinloch still survive. In 1960 a nursery was established at Kinloch to support re-introduction of 20 native tree species, including Scots pine, oak, silver birch, aspen, alder, hawthorn, rowan and holly. Over a million native trees and shrubs have since been planted. The forested area is limited to the environs of Kinloch, the slopes surrounding Loch Scresort and on nearby Meall á Ghoirtein.

As a consequence of high rainfall and acid soils 90 per cent of Rum's vegetation comprises bog and heath. Much of the island is dominated by tussocky purple moor grass and deer sedge. In boggy areas sedges and bog asphodel abound alongside sundew and butterwort. Heather or ling (calluna) occurs in drier areas. The well-fertilised soil beneath the Manx shearwater burrows in the Cuillin keeps the turf green at an unusually high altitude.

Among the island's other flora are the rare arctic sandwort and alpine pennycress, endemic varieties of the heath spotted orchid and eyebright as well as more common species such

Signpost, Kinloch

as blue heath milkwort and roseroot. A total of 590 species of higher plants and ferns have been recorded on Rum.

GETTING AROUND

Visitors are not permitted to bring vehicles to Rum and there is no public transport on the island. Getting around on foot is the norm for most visitors, although mountain bikes can be of use on several of the island's Land Rover tracks.

AMENITIES

The Isle of Rum General Store is situated next to the village hall and stocks bread, fruit and veg, tinned goods, some frozen meat, beers, wines and spirits. Groceries can be pre-ordered with three weeks' notice; tel: 01687 460328. The island's Post Office is at the shop. The village hall has a tearoom – open between 10am and 4pm daily, serving hot drinks, soup, toasted sandwiches and home baking – public

toilets, internet access, a pool table, dart board and a sitting area facing the bay. There is no shelter at the pier.

Kinloch Castle houses the island's hostel and bistro; however at the time of writing (2011) it appears likely that SNH will close the hostel within a few years. The hostel is in the former servants' quarters. Breakfasts, dinners and packed lunches are available. There is a well-equipped communal kitchen for self catering. The bistro is open to non-residents but takes advance bookings only. The Courtyard Bar is open daily from 5pm to 11pm and Sundays 6.30–11pm and serves beers, wine, spirits, soft drinks and savoury snacks. Postcards, castle guidebooks, midge repellent and orchestrion CDs are available for sale at the castle, and in summer there are daily tours of the principal wing of the castle, a time capsule of exotic Edwardiana. Guided tours last an hour and in summer 2011 cost £7 per adult and £3.50 per child.

WALK 1

A round of the Rum Cuillin

Start	Path along the Allt Slugan by Kinloch Castle (NM 402 995)
Distance	27km (17 miles); to Dibidil bothy 18.5km (11½ miles); shorter Hallival and Askival route 11km (7 miles)
Total Ascent	2025m (6645ft); shorter Hallival and Askival route 1220m (4000ft)
Time	9–10hrs (to Dibidil bothy 6–7hrs); shorter Hallival and Askival route 4½–5½hrs
Map	OS Explorer 397: OS Landranger 39

A round of the Rum Cuillin makes for a magnificent and challenging day in the hills and usually features somewhere on the 'to-do' list of Scottish mountain aficionados. A complete round can take ten hours and visits the summits of Barkeval (591m), Hallival (722m), Askival (812m), Trollaval (700m), Ainshval (781m) Sgùrr nan Goibhrean (759m) and Sgùrr nan Gillean (764m). Outlying Ruinsival (528m) can also be included if returning to Kinloch via Harris.

Although providing the finest mountaineering tour in the islands, outside of Skye, the traverse of the Rum Cuillin is nowhere near as difficult as the main ridge of the Black Cuillin of Skye. It requires some moderate scrambling and no climbing other than a couple of short sections that are easily avoided. However, this is not an endeavour to be taken lightly. The route requires a substantial physical effort, involving 2025m of ascent and descent. There are several airy and exposed sections and the weather can change very quickly. While the northernmost hills are formed largely of basalt and gabbro – a coarse-grained rock beloved of climbers and hill walkers for its excellent grip – the fine-grained felsite capping the southern peaks can be slippery in wet conditions.

It is essential that you have a good level of fitness, good navigation skills and are properly equipped before attempting a round of the Rum Cuillin. Ensure that you have plenty of daylight for completing the route and check weather forecasts before setting out; it is not a walk for very wet, windy conditions or poor visibility.

Map continues on
page 46

A stile with a small sign reading 'To the Rum Cuillin' crosses a fence next to the road 100 metres south of **Kinloch Castle**. The path follows the right bank of the Allt Slugan through woodland and past the island's generator before emerging onto rising open ground. ▶

Cross several burns flowing into the river along the way, go through a gateway in an old deer fence and pass a small sluice dam before reaching the **Coire Dubh** at around 270m.

Continue on level ground along the path by the Allt Slugan before arriving at a partially collapsed old stone dam. Cross the river here – this is where the path marked on the OS Explorer map runs out. A short distance ahead, 180 metres above the corrie to the south-west, is the low point of the Bealach Bairc-mheall (466m) between Barkeval and Hallival. The path running directly up to the *bealach* isn't very obvious at first, but it keeps to the left of the burn that tumbles into the corrie.

The path is distinct and easy to follow as it climbs beside the river.

Shortcut via Cnapan Breaca

For those not including Barkeval, a more distinct path skirts around the eastern side of the corrie as it climbs up to the shoulder of the **Cnapan Breaca**. Thereafter the path fades, but it is straightforward to climb south-south-west from here to the *bealach* below Hallival. This route provides no great advantage over climbing directly to the bealach.

From the bealach climb 110m north-west to the first cairn (575m) on the summit ridge of **Barkeval**. The summit proper is over 600 metres west beyond the first cairn. Continue west, passing around a couple of weathered basalt outcrops and pick up a vague path to the summit cairn (591m). ▶

Finding the summit can be tricky in poor visibility.

The **superlative views** south and south-east on to the main peaks of the Rum Cuillin, towering over the Atlantic Corrie, are reason enough to include Barkeval in the traverse. In clear conditions there are fine views south-west down Glen Harris, north-west to the rounded granite hills of Sròn an t-Saighdeir, Orval, Ard Nev and Fionchra and north to the Cuillin of Skye.

Heading east to the Bealach Bairc-mheall, from the summit of Barkeval – Hallival looms above the Atlantic Corrie

Retrace your route to the bealach, then follow the long, steadily rising ridge south-east to **Hallival**. From below, a band of cliffs – formed of a unique variety of gabbro known as allivalite – run around the summit and appear to present something of an obstacle. However, a route through these cliffs can be found without difficulty by keeping to the north-west ridge.

The summit is marked by a cairn and the **views on a clear day** are tremendous, particularly on to Askival and its impressive north ridge. Beyond Askival, the summits of Trollaval, Ainshval, Sgùrr nan Goibhrean and Sgùrr nan Gillean are visible.

From the cairn, continue initially south-west across the summit to begin the 120m descent to the bealach, following a path. To avoid steep crags on the south-east face, descend steeply following the faint path through rocky terrain on the west side of the ridge briefly before trending south-west again to continue down to the bealach. The path climbs a little over a rocky knoll before crossing the bealach and gaining the narrow, grassy north ridge of **Askival**.

Where the ridge arrives beneath the steep crags rising up to the summit on the north and north-west faces of the mountain, at around 650m, follow the path off the ridge as it skirts around Askival's east flank, contouring and rising gradually at first before climbing more steeply and sinuously through rocky terrain to the summit – its upward progress marked by a number of small cairns. Numerous Manx shearwater burrows perforate the grassy slopes between the rock tiers on the mountain's flanks. The summit is marked with a natural stone triangulation pillar encircled by a low shelter wall, and on a clear day the views over to Eigg, Ardnamurchan and Moidart are magnificent. ▸

The Dibidil Horseshoe route (Walk 2) joins the route here.

Alternative shorter walk: Hallival and Askival out and return from Kinloch

Follow the route description above as far as the summit of Askival. Retrace your route back down the north ridge of Askival to the bealach. From the bealach, descend 50m north-west into the Atlantic Corrie to around 550m then contour around beneath Hallival, finally descending around 90m to rejoin the Bealach Bairc-mheall. From the bealach retrace your route into the Coire Dubh then follow the Allt Slugan path back to Kinloch Castle.

From the summit of Askival, descend along the vague path which initially stays in the lee of the west ridge on its south side. As the path descends, it eventually joins the west ridge. The terrain is rocky in places, but the 360m descent to the **Bealach an Oir** (455m) presents no problems.

43

The bealach lies at the head of Glen Dibidil and the **view south-east along the glen** to Eigg, Muck and the mainland beyond is rather fine. On its north side, the bealach drops away into the immense amphitheatre of the Atlantic Corrie with views over to Barkeval and Hallival. To the south-west, forming the western flank of Glen Dibidil, are the imposing triumvirate of Ainshval, Sgùrr nan Goibhrean and Sgùrr nan Gillean.

Escape route

If the weather takes a turn for the worse, then the Bealach an Oir provides you with a good escape route. Descend initially south off the bealach, then bear south-east to keep above the left side of the Dibidil River. Walk closer to the river in its lower reaches. **Dibidil** bothy provides a superb shelter; otherwise follow the pony path back to Kinloch, 8.5km (5 miles) from Dibidil bothy: see below.

From the bealach, climb directly west to gain the east ridge of **Trollaval**. ◄

> There is a fairly distinct path following the ridge, which is useful if you can stay with it.

Climbing the east ridge is initially straightforward, but a little scrambling is required to traverse the craggy terrain encountered between 600m and the mountain's east summit (702m). The slightly higher west summit is about 50m beyond the east summit and a short, steep descent then ascent via a narrow ridge is required to reach it.

> There are **fine views west** from the summit along the Harris Buttress and the Triangular Buttress to Harris Bay beyond. To the south, the imposing bulk of Ainshval looms above the Bealach an Fhuarain.

The route down to the **Bealach an Fhuarain** descends the steep south ridge of Trollaval from the east summit. Care is required as the descent is awkward in places; there is a vague path, but it can be difficult to find its start – especially if visibility is poor. Take care also to avoid descending into the areas of craggy terrain on the mountain's southern flank. From the bealach (520m), pass beneath

Rock window on the Hallival–Askival bealach

the buttress to the west, following a faint path, continue on the path as it climbs to the right (west) of the buttress rising above the south side of the bealach, then crosses a rocky scree slope before gaining the north-east ridge of Ainshval at around 670m. Continue climbing steeply south-west in the lee of the north-east ridge, following a fairly distinct path that skirts above the Grey Corrie before eventually arriving at the cairn-marked summit of **Ainshval** (781m).

From the cairn, follow the path south along the whale-backed summit ridge, which affords some tremendous views in clear conditions. Gradually descend around 100m to a narrow bealach before making the short ascent of Sgùrr nan Goibhrean (759m). From the summit, descend a short way before continuing south-east along

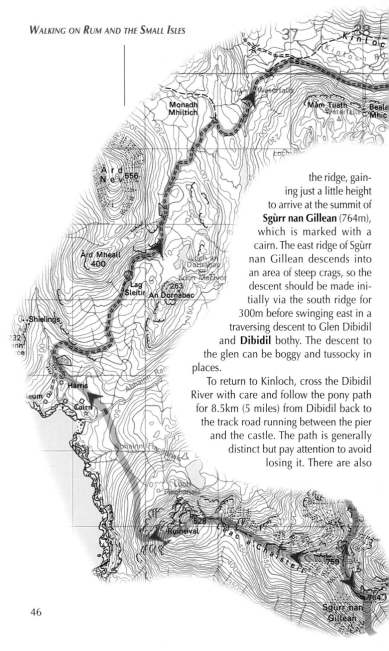

the ridge, gaining just a little height to arrive at the summit of **Sgùrr nan Gillean** (764m), which is marked with a cairn. The east ridge of Sgùrr nan Gillean descends into an area of steep crags, so the descent should be made initially via the south ridge for 300m before swinging east in a traversing descent to Glen Dibidil and **Dibidil** bothy. The descent to the glen can be boggy and tussocky in places.

To return to Kinloch, cross the Dibidil River with care and follow the pony path for 8.5km (5 miles) from Dibidil back to the track road running between the pier and the castle. The path is generally distinct but pay attention to avoid losing it. There are also

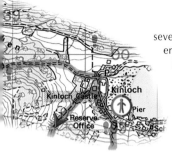

several burns to cross en route, which can be hazardous during wet weather. On reaching the track road, turn left for Kinloch and the castle, turn right for the pier.

Alternative route return route via Ruinsival and Harris

Including rarely-visited Ruinsival in the traverse and returning to Kinloch via Harris Bay adds distance and time to an already demanding route, but it makes for a rewarding alternative. Retrace your steps from Sgùrr nan Gillean to Sgùrr nan Goibhrean and descend west along the broad Leac a' Chaisteal ridge to reach a bealach before climbing 80m to reach the summit of Ruinsival (528m) after 2.2km. In good conditions you'll enjoy grand views, south-east along the rugged coast to Loch Papadil, and north-west across Glen Harris to Harris Bay and the western hills including Orval and Ard Nev.

From the summit, descend initially south-west, then trending west to around 250m. Look out for a large cairn marking the beginning of a path contouring north then north-east into Glen Harris. Follow the path as it descends gradually to cross the Abhainn Fiachanais – find a safe crossing point, then continue north-west to cross the Abhainn Rangail on a substantial wooden bridge. Continue on the track, skirting an impressive raised beach and keeping to the right of some cairns before joining the Kinloch–Harris track (see Walk 7). ▶

Turn right to begin the climb out of Glen Harris and on to Kinloch, which is 10km distant.

There is an excellent bivouac site on the shore at Harris Bay.

WALK 2
The Dibidil Horseshoe

Start	Dibidil bothy (NM 393 927)
Distance	10.5km (6.5 miles) starting/finishing at Dibidil bothy; the walk in/out from Kinloch adds 8.5km each way
Total Ascent	1440m (4720ft)
Time	5–6hrs; the walk in/out from Kinloch adds 3–3½hrs each way
Map	OS Explorer 397: OS Landranger 39

The spectacularly located Dibidil bothy provides the ideal base from which to traverse the horseshoe of peaks flanking wild and remote Glen Dibidil – Beinn nan Stac, Askival, Trollaval, Ainshval, Sgùrr nan Goibhrean and Sgùrr nan Gillean. The horseshoe can be traversed in either direction, although the lesser ascent of Beinn nan Stac (546m) offers an easier start than the steep south-eastern flank of Sgùrr nan Gillean (764m). There are several scrambles on this route, including the south ridge of Askival, which is more difficult than anything encountered on the Rum Cuillin traverse, though this can be avoided. The Dibidil Horseshoe is a magnificent route with some outstanding mountain scenery and spectacular views over the neighbouring islands and mainland mountains

The route in to Dibidil is described in Walk 3, around the coast of Rum.

From Dibidil bothy head back towards Kinloch on the pony path, recrossing the Dibidil River before climbing to around 100m along the flank of **Beinn nan Stac**. Leave the path at NM 400 930 by Cnoc nan Cuilèan to climb north along the mountain's south ridge. Just below the summit there is a short scramble through a line of crags – this can be avoided by continuing north-west to the broad col between Beinn nan Stac and Askival. ◄

From the col, continue climbing north along the south ridge of Askival directly towards the summit. This route makes for moderate to difficult scrambling on good rock for around 250m height over the course of several

To the north-west, Clough's Crag rises up in two tiers towards the Askival Prow below the east ridge.

Map continues on page 50

Scrambling on Askival's south ridge

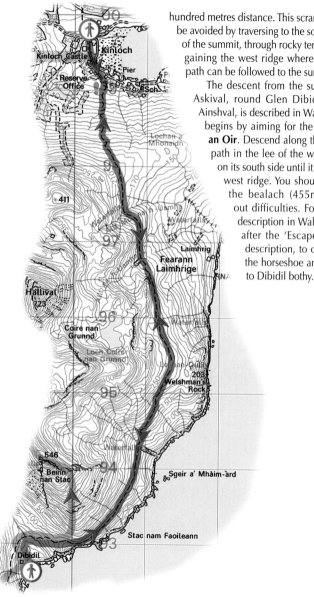

hundred metres distance. This scramble can be avoided by traversing to the south-west of the summit, through rocky terrain, and gaining the west ridge where a vague path can be followed to the summit.

The descent from the summit of Askival, round Glen Dibidil, over Ainshval, is described in Walk 1 and begins by aiming for the **Bealach an Oir**. Descend along the vague path in the lee of the west ridge on its south side until it joins the west ridge. You should reach the bealach (455m) without difficulties. Follow the description in Walk 1 from after the 'Escape Route' description, to complete the horseshoe and return to Dibidil bothy.

WALK 3

Around the coast of Rum

Start	Kinloch
Distance	40km (25 miles)
Total Ascent	2206m (5666ft); via Kilmory and Kinloch glens 2026m (5077ft)
Time	2–3 days
Map	OS Explorer 397: OS Landranger 39

The Rum Cuillin have long been a focal point for walkers. However, Rum also boasts a coastline that is at times spectacular, wild and remote, with high cliffs, rugged, rocky shores, magnificent white sand bays and remarkable geological features. Furthermore, traversing Rum's coastline gives superlative views of the surrounding islands and the mainland mountains and coastline.

A complete circumperambulation of the coastline of Rum only amounts to some 40km (25 miles), but three days is a sensible time to allow as the nature of the terrain makes progress slower and more physically demanding than walking on established footpaths, particularly when carrying camping gear and food.

The fine Mountain Bothies Association (MBA)-maintained **bothies** at Dibidil and Guirdil make for obvious overnight stops along this route, but it is advisable to carry a tent in case you find them fully occupied. Driftwood is scarce – at Dibidil in particular – so it's worth carrying in some kindling and coal if you can. Bothies are simple shelters for all hill-goers to use – please do so responsibly. You can join the Mountain Bothies Association at www.mountainbothies.org.uk.

The section of coastline between Kinloch and Papadil benefits from an old pony path and thereafter stretches of faint path – often deer and goat tracks – aid progress through the wild terrain. The route traverses terrain that is at times boggy, tussocky or covered with dense heather,

Ruin and drystone walled enclosures at Samhnan Insir

but it is nowhere unmanageable except in the very north-east of the island, which this route bypasses in any case.

Drinking water can be collected from the burns which run off the hills at frequent intervals – be sure to collect your water where the stream is visibly moving. You are responsible for carrying your own rubbish out with you. Human waste should always be buried well away from bothies and water sources.

At the end of the 19th century, a guest of George Bullough's, by the name of Harry Hinton, allegedly won a bet that he could run round the island within four hours! This seems wildly implausible.

WARNING

The path between Kinloch and Dibidil can rapidly become impassable due to burns in spate after heavy rain. Do not attempt to cross rivers in spate – if you are swept away your chances of survival are very small. If you manage to cross one river in these conditions you may come up against an impassable torrent further on; if you then attempt to recross the river you previously crossed, you may find that it is running higher and faster than before.

DAY 1
Kinloch to Dibidil

Start	Dibidil pony path, between Loch Scresort ferry slipway and Kinloch Castle (NM 404 991)
Distance	8.5km (5 miles)
Total Ascent	665m (1200ft)
Time	3–3½hrs
Map	OS Explorer 397: OS Landranger 39

The half-day walk out to Dibidil is manageable if you start out directly on arriving by an early ferry. Alternatively a more leisurely start can be made from Kinloch, with plenty of time to explore Glen Dibidil on arrival. Another option is to continue on to Papadil (4½–5½hrs) or Harris Bay (7–8½hrs) – see Day 2 – and bivouac at either of these wonderful spots. For the heroically fit, an early start might allow for walking the Dibidil Horseshoe route from Dibidil bothy (8–9½hrs from Kinloch) – see Walk 2.

From the ferry slipway, follow the track road above the shore of Loch Scresort, to a junction where a signpost indicates the old stone slipway to the right and the castle and other amenities straight ahead. Take neither of these, but instead keep to the left-hand track road for a further 400 metres until just before a set of white-painted estate gates. To the left, the Dibidil pony path begins its gradual climb south. A small sign indicates that Dibidil is 8.5km distant. ▶

The Dibidil pony path extends as far as Papadil and was built in the mid-19th century by the Marquess of Salisbury, then owner of Rum. The path is metalled in places with large stones and small boulders, which aids progress through the wet and boggy terrain. The path is quite distinct, but other than a signpost near the beginning it has no waymarkers. The path can be easy to lose in places – especially when distracted by the fantastic views.

If starting from Kinloch Castle, head south-east along the track road keeping straight ahead at the path junction; pass through the white-painted estate gates and join the start of the Dibidil path to your right shortly after.

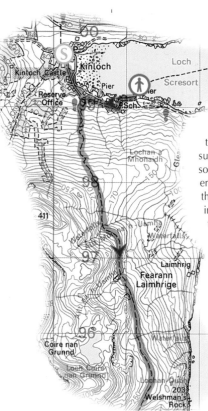

The path climbs steadily to around 200m and, as Loch Scresort drops away behind you, the Black Cuillin of Skye dominate the skyline to your rear (visibility permitting), while Knoydart and Morar form the mountainous boundary to the east. The summit of Hallival is visible to the south-west and mighty Askival soon emerges from its lee. Once at 200m, the path contours for a while, gaining and losing a little height here and there. After nearly 2km the **Allt Mòr na h-Uamha** burn is crossed and after a further 800 metres the **Allt na h-Uamha** is reached – crossing can be tricky if the burn is in spate. Choose your crossing point carefully – if you're not confident, turn back and live to do the walk another day.

Continue contouring along, with Hallival and Askival looming over the **Coire nan Grunnd**, which is above the path to the west. The huge boulders scattered in the corrie were deposited by a glacier, which once flowed from Hallival. After a further 1.5km, as the path passes above **Lochan Dubh**, the view south-east on to the isle of Eigg opens up magnificently – soon the entire island lies before you like a huge basalt comma – and shortly after, the tiny isle of Muck also comes into view. Continue contouring a little further before dropping to 100m in a broad zig-zag to cross the Allt nam Bà by way of a ford across a rock slab. If the burn is in spate, cross via some stones

Map continues on page 55

Crossing a burn on the Dibidil pony path

nearer to the rock pool beneath the narrow fissure in the rock from which the tumbling burn emerges.

Continue around the flank of **Beinn nan Stac** on the 100m contour, and after 1.5km or so the view opens up across to Sgùrr nan Gileann, Sgùrr nan Goibhrean and Ainshval towering above the western side of Glen Dibidil. The path soon begins to descend into Glen Dibidil and the green roof and stone walls of **Dibidil** bothy come into view below the SE flank of Sgùrr nan Gileann. Follow the path down to cross the Dibidil River at a ford, although you may have to cross upstream when the river is in spate. Do so with caution.

If you have the time, energy and inclination, Papadil is a further 4km walk beyond Dibidil and takes between 1½ and 2hrs; Harris Bay is a further 6km and takes an extra 2½–3hrs. There are good opportunities for camping at both sites and

the beaches are good for driftwood. If you are heroically fit and still have at least six or so hours of daylight remaining, you can leave the bulk of your kit at Dibidil bothy and tackle the Dibidil Horseshoe – conditions permitting. See Walk 2.

Built in 1849, **Dibidil bothy** was a ruined shepherd's cottage renovated by an MBA work party in 1970. The story of the Dibidil bothy renovation is recounted in the late Irvine Butterfield's book *Dibidil: A Hebridean Adventure*, first published in 1972 and reprinted by the MBA in 2010.

The bothy has two large rooms, one with a hearth, the other with a woodburning stove. However, there is little driftwood to be gleaned from the shore here. The nearest source is Papadil – a three-hour round-trip. One room has a wide two-tier sleeping platform. The views up Glen Dibidil are magnificent and directly across the Sound of Rum, Eigg lies resplendent with lights from the scattered settlement of Cleadale twinkling after dusk. Beware of deep fissures to the south of the bothy.

Camping by Dibidil bothy

DAY 2
Dibidil to Guirdil

Start	Dibidil bothy (NM 393 927)
Distance	18.5km (11½ miles)
Total Ascent	966m (3170ft)
Time	7½–9hrs
Map	OS Explorer 397: OS Landranger 39

This is the longest and toughest day of this route. There are a number of river crossings to be made, a section of high cliffs to traverse and a steep descent into Glen Guirdil. Much of the route is pathless and it is not recommended during high winds, heavy rain or poor visibility. However, in good or reasonable conditions this is a fine day's walk, taking in some spectacular coastal landscape.

The walk to Papadil from Dibidil is around 4km (2½ miles) and takes 1½–2hrs. From Dibidil bothy, climb around 40m to the 60m contour to the rear of the building to regain the pony path. Most of the way to Papadil the path is quite distinct and easy to follow; however, it is vague in places and it can be easy to lose when admiring the views. The terrain between Dibidil and Papadil is quite complex and boggy – staying on the path greatly assists progress.

The path climbs steadily to around 200m over the course of 1km, then contours along, passing the southern tip of **Loch Dubh an Sgòir**. The path is a little indistinct just before and after the loch. Continue on and shortly begin descending gradually. **Loch Papadil** will begin to emerge below to the north-west as the path descends. ▶

If you plan to camp at Papadil, turn left to skirt around the south-east shore of the loch and cross the outflow to find the best bivouac spots near the beach or above the south-west shore of the loch. Otherwise make for the south-west corner of the small area of woodland, look out

Pay attention here – the path can be easy to lose as it zig-zags on the final stretch down to the loch.

Map continues on page 63

for a rusting iron gate and enter the woodland next to it, rather than attempting to pass around the edge of the loch. Pass through the woodland, which includes some dense rhododendron growth, cross a burn and look out for the eerie, roofless ruins of **Papadil Lodge**.

Papadil Lodge was built as a shooting lodge by John Bullough shortly after he took possession of the island in 1888. Shooting parties would be taken around to the lodge in the estate boat, the servants having already made the journey over from Kinloch by pony.

The ruins of Papadil Lodge

From Papadil Lodge, cross a burn and exit the woods. This is where the path runs out and the landscape ahead looks a formidable prospect, with the flanks of **Leac a Chaisteil** and Ruinsival tumbling precipitously down to the wild and rocky shore. The section between Papadil and Harris Bay should take 2½–3hrs.

Cross another burn at the head of the loch and make for an iron gate. ▶

Go through the gate – there is no fence – pass through a second gate and climb steadily north-west, working your way up to around 120m before contouring along and then around into the broad gully through which the Allt na Gile descends. Keep your height at around 120m or so and cross the burn. Once over, gain a little height and contour along as best as possible, negotiating some rocky terrain, initially at around 150m.

Here there is a good view of the Papadil Pinnacle – a jutting finger of rock standing by the shore at the southern end of the loch.

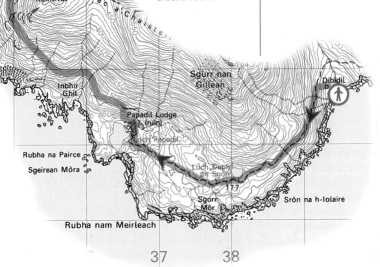

As the terrain allows, gradually gain height over the course of the next kilometre, climbing to around 250m – look out for a large cairn where the south-west flank of **Ruinsival** is turned. The cairn marks the start of a path, which contours initially north around the flank of Ruinsival before descending gradually.

> Here, the **view opens up** along to Harris Bay and the impressive coastline beyond, including the prow of A Bhrìdeanach at Rum's western extremity, with Canna beyond. When free of cloud, the smooth summits of Ard Nev, Orval and Sròn an t-Saighdeir rise to the north-west of Glen Harris.

Follow the path down to cross the **Abhainn Fiachanais** – find a safe crossing point, otherwise follow the river upstream towards the outflow of Loch Fiachanais until you do. The path continues north-west and soon crosses the **Abhainn Rangail** on a substantial wooden bridge. Continue on the track, skirting an impressive raised beach and keeping to the right of some cairns; if the rivers are in spate, continue along the track to cross the Glen Duian River via the bridge, then follow the track to the Mausoleum. Otherwise on passing some dry stone walled enclosures head diagonally (west) towards the shore – you will soon be looking down on an excellent bivouac site in a rectangular enclosure above the beach. If continuing on, cross the outflow of the Glen Duian River and climb a short way to the remarkable Bullough **Mausoleum** – an unlikely Grecian temple perched upon the wild Hebridean shore.

Shorter, tougher alternative
Around 750 metres along the path beyond the cairn, head north-west across country, leaving the path behind. Descend on tussocky ground, using deer paths where possible, and cross a small burn before arriving at the **Abhainn Fiachanais**. Choose your crossing point carefully, especially if the river is running high. Continue for 500 metres to the **Abhainn Rangail** and cross the river

at its outflow across the beach. If this proves tricky there is a footbridge 300 metres upstream. Climb above the bay again and continue beneath the impressive raised beaches for another 400 metres before descending to the beach once again to cross the outflow of the Glen Duian River. Once across, climb a little way to the unmistakable Bullough **Mausoleum**.

The Bullough Mausoleum, Harris Bay

> When John Bullough died in 1891, his remains were interred in an even more ostentatious **Mausoleum** than the present one, which was cut into the rock at the north-western extremity of Harris Bay and included an octagonal stone tower and interior decorated with Italian mosaic tiles.
>
> Allegedly, a tactless guest of Sir George Bullough observed that the Mausoleum was redolent of a public lavatory at Waterloo Station. Sir George had his father's sandstone sarcophagus removed and promptly dynamited the offending structure. John Bullough's remains were finally interred nearby in the neoclassical edifice still standing today, where Sir George and Lady Monica would eventually join him.

In clear conditions there are spectacular views west to the Rum Cuillin.

The section between Harris Bay and Guirdil should take 3½–4½hrs. From the Mausoleum, follow the dry stone wall as it climbs away from the bay. ◄

Once beyond the wall continue north-west, making for the rocky summit of **Gualann na Pairce**. Pass between the twin, rock-scattered peaks (228m and 232m) and continue north-west, soon losing a little height. Pass to the left of a small lochan and cross an area of boggy, hummocky open ground. Steer a course 250 metres inland from the cliff edge. Pass 100 metres to the right of another small lochan close to the cliff edge. Cross a couple of burns, gain a little height and look out for a faint path, which makes the going much easier through the close heather cover.

The path runs closer to the cliff tops, passing near the cliff edge as it reaches the 250m contour. It is more distinct by this point and it's worth staying with it as it climbs to 300m above **Sgorr Reidh**, with views across to the steep, grassy slope sliding down to Wreck Bay. ◄

On a clear day, the views from here along to A' Bhrìdeanach, with Canna, Barra and South Uist beyond, are spectacular.

From Sgorr Reidh the cliff top path runs too close to a very big drop, so climb up towards a large cairn at around 300m, then contour around the flank of **Sròn an t-Saighdeir**, trending north then north-east, following deer paths where you can. Lose some height and pass by the south-east end of spectacle-shaped Spectacle Lochan,

Looking across the A' Bhrìdeanach headland – Rum's westernmost point – with Canna beyond, from Sgorr Reidh

continuing north-east towards **Bealach an Dubh-bhraigh**, between Sròn an t-Saighdeir and **Bloodstone Hill**. Cross the open ground of the bealach and pass a small lochan as the view on to Glen Guirdil opens up, with Fionchra to the north-east and the towering cliffs of Orval looming above the head of the glen to the east.

From here there are two choices. The best option is to head north-west, along the north-east flank of Bloodstone Hill, losing only a little height initially. There are vague traces of path here, which stay above areas of scree on the steep slope. Keep contouring at around 240m for 600 metres or so, then descend steadily along a path to cross two burns descending gullies at obvious points around 140m. Once over, descend very steeply on a grassy slope heading for the south-east corner of a deer-fenced plantation. Once down, continue along the east side of the plantation, then follow the track above the Guirdil River down to the beach, crossing the outflow wherever is easiest to arrive at Guirdil bothy.

Alternative Glen Guirdil route

Alternatively, it is possible to descend along the burn flowing into the glen from the small lochan, which converges with the Guirdil River near the floor of the glen. Continue along the river's edge for

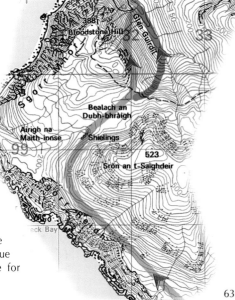

Bloodstone Hill rearing above Guirdil bothy

1.5km, crossing several burns, before reaching Guirdil Bay and the bothy. The terrain makes for tough going, however, and it is not a route for wet weather when the rivers are in spate.

> **Guirdil bothy** is a former shepherd's cottage, built in 1848 and renovated by the MBA. It is a fine bothy in a remarkable location, perched above the shore at the mouth of Glen Guirdil beneath the steep flanks of Bloodstone Hill with fine views across the sound to Sanday and Canna.
>
> Guirdil Bay is the site of a former crofting settlement, but the discovery of prehistoric burial cairns here indicates much earlier human occupation. These early settlers were attracted to the site by a seam of **bloodstone**, a crystalline green agate flecked with red spots of oxidised jasper, which gives Creag nan Stardean – the lava-capped hill towering above Guirdil – its common name. Bloodstone could be worked to make tools including knives and scrapers as well as arrow heads. Examples of such artefacts originating on Rum have been found far and wide throughout the Hebrides. Fragments still break off from the seam on the face

of Bloodstone Hill and can be picked up on the slopes and the beach below the summit.

A kilometre north-east of Guirdil bothy, beneath the cliffs where the Glen Shellesder Burn cascades to the shore by way of a fine waterfall, there is a remarkable stretch of coastline full of impressive geological features including subterranean tunnels, cavernous caves and a huge rock arch. This area is really worth exploring from Guirdil bothy and is also the most likely source of driftwood in the vicinity.

DAY 3
Guirdil Bothy to Kinloch via Kilmory Bay

Start	Guirdil bothy (NG 319 013)
Distance	15km (9¼ miles); via Kilmory and Kinloch glens 14km (8¾ miles)
Total Ascent	575m (1885ft); via Kilmory and Kinloch glens 395m (1296m)
Time	5½–6½hrs; via Kilmory and Kinloch glens 5–6hrs
Map	OS Explorer 397: OS Landranger 39

This day's walk starts along a good path to Glen Shellesder, then a fainter one as far as Kilmory, the island's red deer research HQ. It is worth exploring the few kilometres of wonderful coastline beyond Kilmory Bay but there is little to gain from attempting to walk around to Kinloch along the final north-eastern stretch of coastline: a few kilometres east of Kilmory the coastal terrain becomes very boggy, tussocky and difficult to negotiate, and beyond the beach at Samhnan Insir the fine scenery recedes.

Instead there are two options: continue over Mullach Mòr (304m) from Samhnan Insir to Kinloch – this route is best suited to clear conditions as the terrain is complex and can be rough in places – or turn around, return to Kilmory Bay to follow the Land Rover track up along Kilmory Glen then down Kinloch Glen to Kinloch.

To the rear of the bothy, a rusted iron gate frame heralds the beginning of a path, which continues parallel to the river a short way before zig-zagging east up to around 70m on to then along the cliff tops. The path is quite distinct and winds its way with a little up and down for 1km over to Glen Shellesder. The path arrives at a ford across the **Glen Shellesder Burn**, but it is often deep at this point. There is an easier crossing point 75 metres upstream – but take care on the slippery rocks. In very wet weather, attempting to cross the Glen Shellesder Burn **can be dangerous**. In this case it may be best to return to Kinloch via Glen Guirdil and the Bealach a' Bhràigh Bhig (see Walk 6).

The path continues up Glen Shellesder alongside the burn, but leave it here, climbing away from the burn and continuing northeast across country, gaining some height. Follow deer paths where possible, as the terrain is boggy in places. Make for a pillow lava outcrop atop a rise, descend a little across open ground then climb a little again, making for a rocky spur. Skirt around this then descend to follow an obvious deer path across an area of boggy open ground. Follow the path where possible – it is vague in places, but very useful through the heather and boggy ground – and contour along above the cliff tops at 80–90m for the next 2km, crossing several burns cascading down to the cliffs along the way; these are easy enough to cross, especially if you manage to follow the faint path.

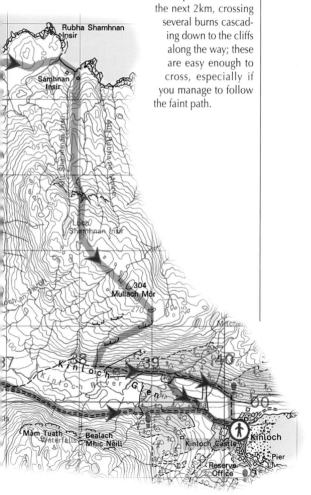

There is some **splendid coastal scenery** to admire along this stretch, including impressive cliffs, beautiful bays, waterfalls and rock stacks, with fine views north-east to the Black Cuillin of Skye – conditions permitting.

After 2km **Kilmory** Lodge – the red deer survey HQ – will come into view. Descend towards a small bay, using deer paths where possible. Skirt around the bay, then cut across the open ground in front of Kilmory Lodge. Join the Land Rover track that runs to the rear of the lodge and follow it south for 100 metres before following a vague path east to the Kilmory River. If the tide permits cross the river's outflow, otherwise follow it upstream a short way to cross at a footbridge, then continue beneath the marram grass-covered dunes and onto the beautiful two-tone red and white sand expanse of Kilmory Bay.

Shipwrecked trawler near Kilmory Bay

From the eastern end of Kilmory Bay, climb a short way where a sloping outcrop of rock eases up from the

Ruin at Samhnan Insir

beach. Stay just above the shore before descending again to pass a small rocky beach. Continue past a series of remarkable rock formations then steer a course around the heads of a couple of narrow gorges. The ground can be quite boggy here, so follow deer tracks and continue across an area of open ground, turning south-east before emerging at the western end of **Samhnan Insir**. Walk along the beautiful sandy beach to the ruined homestead at the south-eastern end of the bay. From here, either retrace your steps to Kilmory Bay, recross the Kilmory River then return to Kinloch via the Land Rover tracks through Kilmory and Kinloch glens, or take the following route over Mullach Mòr to join the Kinloch Glen track directly.

Easy return via Kilmory and Kinloch Glens
Head south for 4.5km along the Kilmory track before intersecting with the Kinloch–Harris track. Turn left (east) and continue for 3.5km to Kinloch.

Pass the ruined homestead at the south-eastern end of the bay, cross a gully, climb to the right of several large dry stone walled enclosures and continue directly south up on to the ridge climbing gently above and east of the Allt Samhnan Insir. ▶

The terrain is not rough here and deer paths aid progress through the heather.

At around 150m, a kilometre or so south of Samhnan Insir, contour around a little to the south-west to meet the **Allt Samhnan Insir** and follow the left bank of the burn up through the narrow glen. Where the ground steepens, climb around to the east a little to find the easiest route up through the rocky terrain. Where the ground levels to the east of **Loch Shamhnan Insir**, at around 270m, look out for the 'Vanessa' triangulation pillar on **Mullach Mòr** (304m) a kilometre distant to the south-east. Carefully work a route through the terrain of rocky outcrops, small lochans and tussocky grass to the summit, which lies just above and south-east of Boat House Loch.

From the summit, descend initially south-east, then south then south-west, keeping to the exposed rock of the ridges tumbling down to **Kinloch Glen** – avoid the terrain between the ridges, which is very hard going through long tussocky grass over uneven ground. Make for the western end of a woodland plantation sitting above the north side of the **Kinloch River**. A ladder stile crosses the deer fence into the plantation, where a boggy footpath contours along the glen. After about 1km, turn off the old path onto a metalled path that descends to the river which it follows briefly before crossing via a ford (when the river is low) or a footbridge. Follow the path to join the main Kinloch Glen track and continue east into Kinloch.

Alternative woodland route

Alternatively, on entering the plantation, continue contouring along the glen for 2km before turning right through a gate, descending along the edge of a paddock and through another gate. Turn left to a crossroads then right to continue to Kinloch Castle.

WALK 4
Kinloch to Guirdil

Start	Kinloch Castle (NM 402 995)
Distance	10.5km (6½ miles) each way; via Glen Shellesder: 9.6km (6 miles) each way
Total Ascent	415m (1360ft); via Glen Shellesder 296m (970m)
Time	3–3½hrs each way
Map	OS Explorer 397: OS Landranger 39

This route leads across Rum to Guirdil, where there's a fine MBA bothy in a remarkable location. There's an alternative, more sheltered route through Glen Shellesder which can be used as a return route. However, in wet weather the route through Glen Shellesder can be very boggy and difficult: there are several fords and attempting to cross the Glen Shellesder Burn can be dangerous. The route via the Bealach a' Bhràigh Bhig is the best option both ways in such conditions.

The first section, from Kinloch to the Bealach a' Bhràigh Bhig, takes 2–2½hrs. From Kinloch Castle follow the track north for 200 metres, then turn left to follow the track west along the south side of the Kinloch River. The Kinloch Glen track climbs gradually to 100m then contours along, passing the waterfalls cascading down from Loch Bealach Mhic Neill after 2.3km. A further kilometre brings you to a fork in the track.

Continue along the left-hand fork – the right-hand track leads to Kilmory Bay and to the alternative route to/from Guirdil down Glen Shellesder. The track soon passes above the ruins of Salisbury's Dam then climbs gradually to 180m before arriving at Malcolm's Bridge, 1.75km beyond the Kinloch–Kilmory path junction. Leave the track to follow the footpath, originally a pony path, heading initially north along the Abhainn Monadh Mhiltich. The path soon trends west, crossing and re-crossing the burn – this can be a boggy experience during

Orval's imposing cliffs dominate the head of Glen Guirdil

wet weather, although the path is metalled with stone and timbers in some sections. The path begins to climb, gradually at first then

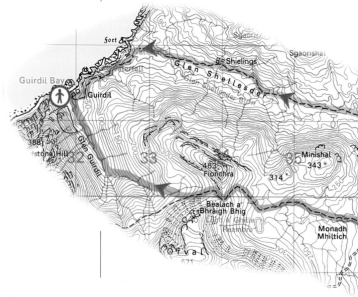

more steeply, arriving at the **Bealach a' Bhràigh Bhig** (370m) after 2.5km.

From the bealach, follow the pony path initially north-west as it gently descends into, then contours west around the head of, **Glen Guirdil**, beneath the towering cliffs of Orval's northern flank. After around 500 metres, leave the path and head directly down into the glen. Follow the vague path if possible. After 200 metres or so, cross a small burn and keep to the right of a larger burn feeding into the Guirdil River. After 1km, pass to the right of a fenced wooded enclosure as the terrain drops more steeply towards the river. At around 100m, join the path contouring along above the river; continue along the path, which can be boggy in places, for 1km to arrive at **Guirdil Bay** and the bothy. From the bealach to the bothy takes around 1hr–1hr 15mins.

To return to Kinloch, retrace your outward route or reverse the alternative outward route via Glen Shellesder – except in wet weather, when this is not a good option.

Alternative outward route via Glen Shellesder
The walk from Kinloch to the turnoff for this route takes 1hr–1hr 20mins; the Glen Shellesder path takes between 1½–1¾hrs. At the Kinloch–Kilmory Land Rover track junction, where the main route to the Bealach a' Bhràigh Bhig forks left, turn right to follow the Kilmory track as it descends a little and soon begins

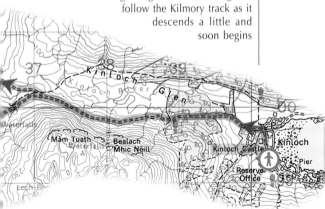

Looking back to the coast at the mouth of Glen Shellesder

to swing north. After 1km, join the Glen Shellesder path as it climbs gradually away from the left-hand side (north-east) of the Kilmory track. The path soon passes by a coniferous forestry plantation and after 1km crosses the watershed between **Sgaorishal** and **Minishal** at around 135m, before beginning the gradual descent through **Glen Shellesder**. ◄

The path is quite distinct, but it can be boggy in places and there are several fords, though these are only an issue in wet weather.

A ford crosses the river just before it descends to the shore via a waterfall; however, it is nearly always too deep to cross here. Instead, cross 75 metres upstream – be careful as the rocks are very slippery. The path continues south-west along the coast for 1km and is easy to follow, but it is possible to mislay it before descending to **Guirdil Bay**; however, the bothy is soon visible below and it is easy to find a route down to it. This last section takes around 20mins. To return to Kinloch, retrace your outward route or reverse the outward route via the Bealach a' Bhràigh Bhig (see Walk 6 for route description).

WALK 5

The Guirdil Horseshoe

Start	Guirdil bothy NG 319 013
Distance	9km (5½ miles) to 14.5km (9 miles); walk to/from Kinloch adds 10.5km (6½ miles) each way
Total Ascent	708m (2325ft); Bloodstone Hill adds 159m (523ft); Ard Nev adds 220m (720ft)
Time	3–3½hrs to 4½–5½hrs; add 3–3½hrs each way to/from Kinloch (see Walk 4)
Map	OS Explorer 397: OS Landranger 39

This is a fine half-day walk – with longer variants – taking in some or all of the principal peaks of Rum's often overlooked north-west – Bloodstone Hill, Sròn an t-Saighdeir, Orval, Ard Nev and Fionchra. Each of these hills offers remarkable views across Rum and the neighbouring islands; the views of Canna from Bloodstone Hill and the Rum Cuillin from Ard Nev are particularly fine.

These whale-backed granite and lava-capped hills are a less demanding proposition than their loftier cousins which dominate the island's southern skyline, though the terrain is challenging in places. Walk 6 provides an alternative itinerary for visiting these hills as an out and return route from Kinloch.

From the bothy, drop down to cross the **Guirdil River** where it is fordable (do not attempt when river is in spate). Head south-east back up the glen next to the river, initially on a track passing beneath a wooded enclosure. At the south-east corner of the enclosure, begin to climb steeply up the north-east flank of Bloodstone Hill on a pathless grassy slope. Cross two shallow, dry gullies, continue climbing then in quick succession cross two burns flowing down gullies at obvious crossing points at around 140m. Continue climbing, less steeply, along the flank of the hill to about 250m, then follow traces of an old path, which contours around the hillside, to gain the **Bealach**

Setting off on the Guirdil Horseshoe, with Bloodstone Hill dominating the scene

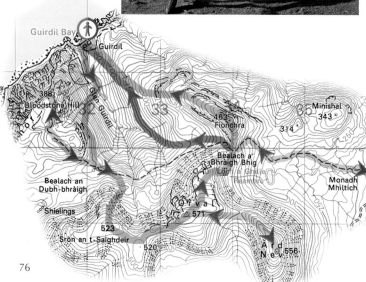

an Dubh-bhràigh (260m). Near a small lochan, join the old pony path that winds its course from Malcolm's Bridge, over the Bealach a' Bhràigh Bhig and around the head of Glen Guirdil to Bloodstone Hill.

Ascent of Bloodstone Hill

To include **Bloodstone Hill** in your itinerary, turn right (north-west) along the pony path and soon begin climbing steadily. After climbing 100m the path drops a little, crossing boggy ground before climbing again to reach the pillow lava-capped summit.

Exercise caution as the summit drops away to sheer cliffs on the hill's north-west flank. The views on a clear day are spectacular; Canna and Sanday lie supine across the Sound of Canna with Barra and South Uist beyond; while the jagged profile of Skye's Black Cuillin frames the horizon to the north-east. Retrace your steps to the bealach. ▶

This ascent adds 2.5km (1½ miles) and takes around 40mins.

From the lochan on Bealach an Dubh-bhràigh, follow the pony path south-east for around 400 metres as it skirts around the head of the valley before leaving the path to climb quite steeply a little west of south along the pathless north ridge of **Sròn an t-Saighdeir**. The 275-metre climb on an even, steepish gradient over moderately

Climbing along the steep flank of Bloodstone Hill with Guirdil Bay and the bothy far below

rough, boggy, tussocky, rock-strewn, terrain is not the most enjoyable of climbs, but it presents no difficulties.

The broad, boulder-strewn summit plateau of Sròn t-Saighdeir (523m) is marked with a cairn and there are fine views along the ridge to Orval and the Rum Cuillin to the south. From the summit cairn, continue south-east then north-east along the grassy ridge, with a little up and down before climbing a short way to the rounded summit of **Orval**, which is marked with a cairn and a 'Vanessa' triangulation pillar. To the south-east across a bealach stands Ard Nev, a lovely whale-backed hill. ◄

Ard Nev provides probably the best views on to the Rum Cuillin to be found anywhere on the island.

Ascent of Ard Nev

To include Ard Nev in your itinerary, continue east from the summit cairn on Orval, soon descending steadily down an even slope with steeply rising ground to your left, arriving on the bealach after about 750 metres. From the bealach, climb directly along the whale-backed ridge of **Ard Nev** to arrive at the summit cairn after a further 750 metres. Retrace your steps to the summit of Orval. This variant adds 3km (2 miles) to the route and takes around 1hr.

In clear conditions there are impressive views down Glen Guirdil and along the cliffs of Orval's north-west face.

From the summit of Orval, continue initially north-east then north along the ridge. ◄

Where the ridge descends to the north-east it runs into craggy terrain; to avoid this, turn right (east) and descend steeply a short way before bearing north-east to descend the last 250 metres to the **Bealach a' Bhràigh Bhig** (370m) between Orval and Fionchra. The pony path from Malcolm's Bridge to Bloodstone Hill crosses the bealach and provides an alternative route for returning to Guirdil bothy (see below); following this path the other way will return you to Kinloch.

Fionchra is a fine outpost for superlative views across Rum and beyond, especially the towering cliffs of Orval's north-west face.

From the bealach climb gently north-east for 200m before turning north-west and climbing more steeply to the distinctive cupola-shaped summit of **Fionchra** (463m); the short, straightforward climb takes around 15mins. ◄

From the summit of Fionchra, descend north-west along the spine of the hill to around 350m. From here, descend more steeply west into **Glen Guirdil** to avoid

the crags above Coire na Loigh. The ground is tussocky
and boggy in places and hard going until you reach the
old path contouring above the river at around 100m.
Follow the path, which can be boggy in places, for the
remaining 1km back to **Guirdil** bothy. The return from
the Bealach a' Bhràigh Bhig to Guirdil bothy via Fionchra
takes 1¼–1½hrs.

*Fionchra (left) and
Orval seen from the
north ridge of Sròn an
t-Saighdeir*

Shortcut from Bealach a' Bhràigh Bhig to Guirdil bothy
Follow the route description in paragraph three of Walk
4. This variant is slightly quicker than the Fionchra route
(1–1¼hrs) and avoids the rough descent along the flank
of Fionchra.

WALK 6
Around Rum's western hills

Start	Kinloch Castle (NM 402 995)
Distance	25.5km (16 miles); shorter alternatives are available
Total Ascent	1341m (4402ft); Bloodstone Hill only 907m (2978ft)
Time	Up to 8–9hrs, plus ½hr with ascent of Fionchra
Map	OS Explorer 397: OS Landranger 39

The Rum Cuillin may edge the island's western hills for all-round mountain drama, but there is some fine walking amid this less-frequented hinterland. Furthermore, the western hills provide grand views across Rum and the neighbouring islands – in particular, the views onto Canna and Sanday from Bloodstone Hill and the Rum Cuillin from Orval and Ard Nev are spectacular in clear conditions.

Though these routes present no real difficulties to fit walkers, walking the whole of this route makes for a very long day's walk when breaks are factored in, and there is some rough and pathless terrain. The whole route should only be attempted by very strong walkers when sufficient daylight is available: shorter alternatives are included in the route description below.

A shorter walk, just taking in Orval and Ard Nev from the bealach, is 19.5km (12 miles) return from Kinloch and takes 7–8hrs.

From Kinloch Castle to the **Bealach a' Bhràigh Bhig**, follow the route description in the first two paragraphs of Walk 4. This section takes 2–2½hrs. From here the walk carries on to Bloodstone Hill and then back via Orval and Ard Nev. ◄

> From the bealach it's a short, straightforward 15mins climb north-east then north-west to the distinctive cupola-shaped summit of **Fionchra** (463m), with fine views across Rum, especially onto the towering cliffs of Orval's north-west face.

Orval from Fionchra

From the Bealach a' Bhràigh Bhig, continue initially north-west then south-west along the pony path, steadily descending to around 250m and then contouring along with a little up and down beneath the impressive cliffs of Orval's north-west face. ▶

There are impressive views down the glen, over to Canna and north-west to Bloodstone Hill. After 2km the path arrives on the **Bealach an Dubh-bhràigh** (260m) and soon passes a small lochan.

Continue north-west along the pony path and soon begin climbing steadily up on to the pillow lava-capped

You should be able to pick out the needle-like 30-metre Orval Pinnacle thrusting skywards just in front of the cliff-face.

Map continues on page 83

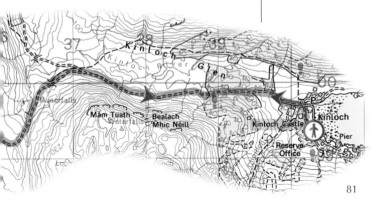

Descending by the Abhainn Monadh Mhiltich from the Bealach a' Bhràigh-bhig

If returning directly to Kinloch, rather than continuing on to Orval and Ard Nev, simply retrace your outward route, for a total route of 21km (13 miles) and 5–6hrs.

hilltop. After climbing 100m the path drops a little, crossing boggy ground before climbing again to reach the summit.

Exercise caution as the summit drops away to sheer cliffs on the hill's north-west flank. The views on a clear day are spectacular; Canna and Sanday lie supine across the Sound of Canna with Barra and South Uist beyond, while the jagged profile of Skye's Black Cuillin frames the horizon to the north-east. ◄

Excursion to Guirdil Bay
If you want to detour via Guirdil Bay and the bothy, retrace your steps to the bealach and follow the main route description from paragraph 11 at the end of Walk 3, Day 2. To return to Kinloch from Guirdil Bay, retrace your route to the **Bealach an Dubh-bhràigh**, or from the rear of the bothy follow the path running up through **Glen Guirdil**, initially parallel to the **Guirdil River** above its left bank. The path can be boggy in places. Where it peters out, after 1km at around 100m, continue uphill on tussocky ground past a wooded enclosure then continue climbing south-east steadily for 1km, keeping left of the burn, to rejoin the pony path. Retrace the outward route over the **Bealach a Bhràigh Bhig** and on to Kinloch.

To continue the main route, from the lochan on the **Bealach an Dubh-bhràigh** follow the pony path south-east for around 400m as it skirts around the head of the valley before leaving the track to climb quite steeply a little west of south along the pathless north-east ridge of Sròn an t-Saighdeir. The 275m climb on an even, steepish gradient over moderately rough – boggy, tussocky, rock strewn – terrain is not the most enjoyable of climbs, but it presents no difficulties.

The broad, boulder-strewn summit plateau of **Sròn t-Saighdeir** (523m) is marked with a cairn and there are fine views along the ridge to Orval and the Rum Cuillin to the south. From the summit cairn, continue initially south-east then north-east along the grassy ridge, with a little up and down before climbing a short way to the rounded summit of **Orval**, which is marked with a cairn and a 'Vanessa' pillar triangulation point. To the south-east, across a bealach, stands Ard Nev, a lovely whale-backed hill, which provides probably the best views on to the Rum Cuillin to be found anywhere on the island, and so demands a visit.

From the summit cairn on Orval, descend steadily eastwards down an even-gradiented slope with steeply rising ground to your left, arriving on the bealach after about 750 metres. From the bealach, climb directly along the whale-backed ridge of **Ard Nev** to arrive at the summit cairn after a further 750 metres. Retrace your steps to the summit of Orval (omitting Ard Nev from your itinerary saves 3km and around 1hr).

From the summit of Orval, continue initially north-east then north along the ridge. ◀

Where the ridge descends to the north-east it runs into craggy terrain: to avoid this, turn right (east) and descend steeply a short way before bearing north-east to descend the last 250 metres to the **Bealach a Bhràigh Bhig** (370m) between Orval and Fionchra. From here you can return directly to Kinloch by the outward route or, if you haven't already, make the short climb of Fionchra.

In clear conditions there are impressive views down Glen Guirdil and along the cliffs of Orval's north-west faces.

WALK 7

Kinloch to Kilmory Bay or Harris

Start	Kinloch Castle (NM 402 995)
Distance	Kinloch to Kilmory Bay 16km (10 miles) return; Kinloch to Harris Bay 21.5km (13½ miles) return
Total Ascent	Kinloch–Harris Bay 340m (1115ft) each way; Kinloch–Kilmory Bay 185m (607ft) each way
Time	Kinloch to Kilmory Bay 5–5½hrs return; Kinloch to Harris Bay 6–6½hrs return
Map	OS Explorer 397: OS Landranger 39

These are straightforward, easy to follow routes on extensively-metalled Land Rover tracks. The route most walkers will do is to the Bullough Mausoleum at Harris, which is the main route described here, but the alternative Kilmory walk has its attractions too. The tracks themselves would make for dull walking were it not for the fine views of the island's mountainous hinterland along the way. Both Kilmory and Harris Bays are wonderful places to arrive at and reward exploration, while also providing access to fine sections of Rum's coastline. Both routes are negotiable for most of their lengths by mountain bike. The wildlife spotting opportunities are also excellent.

The main draw at Harris is the Bullough family Mausoleum and views west to the Rum Cuillin: Kilmory has the HQ of Rum's red deer research programme at Kilmory Lodge, and a beautiful piece of coastline stretching eastwards as far as Samhnan Insir.

Looking along the Harris Bay track to the Rum Cuillin (photo: James Boulter)

Map continues on
page 88

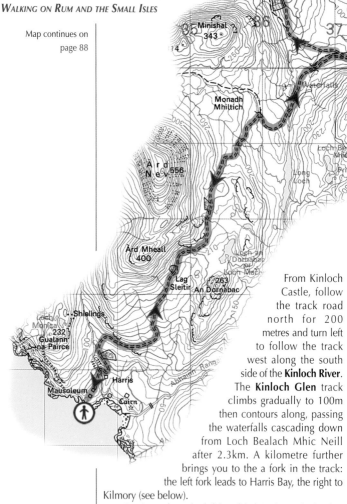

From Kinloch
Castle, follow
the track road
north for 200
metres and turn left
to follow the track
west along the south
side of the **Kinloch River**.
The **Kinloch Glen** track
climbs gradually to 100m
then contours along, passing
the waterfalls cascading down
from Loch Bealach Mhic Neill
after 2.3km. A kilometre further
brings you to the a fork in the track:
the left fork leads to Harris Bay, the right to
Kilmory (see below).

Continue along the left-hand fork in the Kinloch Glen
track. A short way further on the track passes above the
ruins of Salisbury's Dam then climbs gradually to 180m
before arriving at Malcolm's Bridge 1.75km beyond the
Kinloch–Kilmory path junction. Continuing south-west,

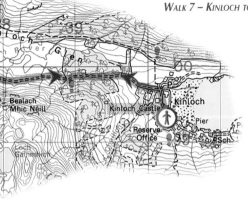

the track climbs more steeply to about 250m as it passes beneath Ard Nev. The track then loses some height before contouring beneath Ard Mheall then winding more steeply downhill **Harris**. Cross the bridge over the Glen Duian River and continue past Harris Lodge to the Bullough **Mausoleum** (see Walk 3, Day 2). The spectacular bay, with its magnificent raised beach and plentiful wildlife is well worth exploring. The 250m climb out of Harris on the way back makes itself felt.

Alternative walk to Kilmory Bay
Continue initially north-west along the right-hand track, which soon descends a little then swings north. The track, which is metalled with pebbles for much of its length, is easy to follow and descends very gradually over the course of 4.5km to **Kilmory**. Around 100 metres before reaching

Looking south along the Kilmory Glen track (photo: Peter Khambatta)

Rum's red deer, the subject of long-term research into the species' sociobiology and behavioural ecology (photo: Konrad Borkowski)

Kilmory Lodge, turn right off the track and follow a vague path east to the Kilmory River.

Kilmory Lodge is the headquarters of Edinburgh and Cambridge Universities' red deer survey, and a number of deer can generally be found here year round, especially during the rut from September to November, when the stags come down from the hills to fight for mating rights.

If the tide permits, cross the river's out-flow, otherwise cross the footbridge a short way upstream then continue beneath the marram grass-covered dunes and along the beautiful red–white sand expanse of Kilmory Bay. It is worth exploring the few kilometres of wonderful coastline east of Kilmory before either returning to Kinloch by your outward route, or heading over Mullach Mòr to join the Kinloch Glen track directly (see Walk 3, Day 3).

EIGG
Eige

Walkers on the summit of An Sgùrr (Walk 8)

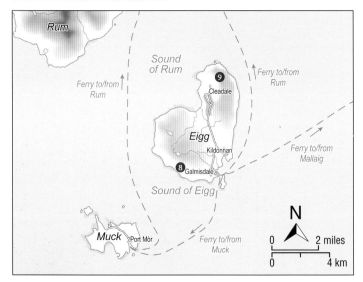

Dùghall Mòr nan Eilean surveys the scene from An Sgùrr (Walk 8)

INTRODUCTION

Eigg seen from the MV Lochnevis

Eigg, second largest of the Small Isles, lies a little less than 7km (4¼ miles) south-east of Rum, 11km to the south of Skye, and 7.5km north of the Ardnamurchan peninsula. Eigg is 9km (5½ miles) from north to south, 5km (3 miles) east to west and has an area of 31km² (12 square miles). Eigg boasts the most varied scenery of the Small Isles and also has a diverse range of wildlife habitats. Much of the island is managed by the Scottish Wildlife Trust (SWT), with the remit of nurturing the indigenous flora and fauna and increasing the island's biodiversity in the long term.

The island's obvious draw for walkers is An Sgùrr, Eigg's distinctive pitchstone summit, which is sheer on three sides and rises to 393m. In clear conditions the summit of An Sgùrr provides fine 360° views, taking in the surrounding islands and the mountains of the mainland. However, there is more to walking on Eigg than An Sgùrr. The routes in this guide take in diverse landscapes including a moorland plateau, white sand bays, basalt cliffs, rocky coastline and abandoned settlements.

Eigg is the historic capital of the Small Isles Parish and has the largest population of the island group, with 86 permanent residents in 2010: consequently the island has more accommodation and other amenities than the other Small Isles. Known as the Jewel of the Hebrides, its fertile pastures, sheltered bays and mild climate have long marked Eigg as an attractive

Looking up to the sheer south face of An Sgùrr from the Grulin path (Walk 8)

site for settlement, with human occupation of the island dating back 8000 years. However, Eigg's history has often been bloody and turbulent with massacres, forced migration and feckless owners visited on the islanders over the centuries.

Eigg's fortunes have improved in recent years, since the island was bought by the Isle of Eigg Heritage Trust (IEHT), a partnership of islanders, the Highland Council and the SWT. With the buy-out in 1997, the islanders took control of their future, bringing to a close decades of mismanagement by absentee landlords. Notably, the Eigg community has become a hotbed of environmental endeavour, implementing successful sustainable energy production and biodiversity development.

The harbour, pier, ferry terminal and main anchorage are situated at Galmisdale at the island's south-east

corner. The grocery shop, post office, craft shop and tea room are all located near the pier and several scatterings of houses are found in the vicinity at Galmisdale, Sandavore and Kildonan. The main settlement is Cleadale, a fertile coastal plain on the island's northwest coast.

The centre of the island is a moorland plateau, rising to 393m (1289ft) at An Sgùrr, Eigg's distinctive, prow-like pitchstone summit. In fine weather, the summit of An Sgùrr offers spectacular 360° views of Rum, Coll, Muck, the Outer Hebrides, Skye, Ardnamurchan and the mountains of Lochaber on the mainland.

GEOLOGY

Eigg and its neighbour, Muck, are both largely formed of lava flows of Tertiary age, which are the remnants of what was once a much larger lava field, erupted from a volcano slightly older than Rum. These lava flows are evident in the step-like features clearly visible on both islands; the small escarpments were formed from the hard, slow-cooling core of each flow, while the gentler slopes between are composed of the softer, more easily eroded rock formed above and below the core.

The pitchstone ridge of An Sgùrr, which gives Eigg its distinctive profile, provides evidence of the final phases of volcanic activity in this area of Scotland. Thick flows of basalt lava had previously been erupted, forming a harsh and inhospitable landscape. Lying in a valley on top of these lavas, layers of conglomerates containing water-rounded pebbles reveal the course of an ancient river bed.

As volcanic activity in the area drew to a close, a nearby volcano erupted lava of an unusual, sticky composition, which flowed along this ancient water course. The lava cooled gradually, forming remarkable hexagonal columns dozens of metres high, reminiscent of the basalt columns of the Giant's Causeway on the Antrim coast and Fingal's Cave on the Hebridean island of Staffa. Being harder than the surrounding rock, erosion has left the pitchstone eminence of An Sgùrr in its elevated position.

The formation of the extensive inland cliff round the whole northern part of Eigg is due to the slipping of the basalt mass of Beinn Bhuidhe on the underlying sediments. Beneath

The basalt cliffs forming the eastern flank of the Beinn Bhuidhe plateau (Walk 9) (photo: Peter Khambatta)

the basalts are a series of sandstones, limestones and shales formed during the Jurassic period. These form the low ground running round the coast from Kildonan in the south-east to Laig in the north-west.

Glaciation removed much of the pre-glacial soil from the island, except for small quantities of boulder clay. However, rapid weathering of the basalt rock combined with wind blown sand has produced excellent loam soils, albeit deficient in phosphate. The phenomenon of the 'singing sands' of Tràigh a' Bhìgeil at Cleadale is attributable to the uniform size of the quartz grains which form them: the sands only 'sing' when dry.

HISTORY

Neolithic axe heads have been recovered on Eigg and cairn-marked graves span the long period between the Neolithic and Bronze Ages. Several Bronze Age farms provide evidence of continuing settlement, and there are several Iron Age duns (forts) on the island, including one impressively located on An Sgùrr and another at Rubha na Crannaig.

Towards the end of the sixth century a monastery was founded at Kildonan by St Donnan, a Celtic Christian missionary from Ireland. However, Donnan's presence eventually provoked the wrath of the local Pictish queen, who massacred the entire monastic community in 617. St Donnan is believed to have been buried on the island. After his death, the monastery came under Iona's rule and subsequently flourished. Several Early Christian crosses recovered at Kildonan attest to the monastery's importance at the time.

Eigg was subjected to Viking raids from early in the eighth century, but the Norsemen eventually settled here and used the island as a base for trading with Ireland and beyond. As well as physical traces, evidence of the Norse settlement is apparent in island

Ruins at Grulin, looking over to the isle of Muck (Walk 8)

place-names, such as Galmisdale, Cleadale and 'Eigg' itself, which derives from an Old Norse word meaning 'hollow' or 'notch', referring to the island's low-lying middle.

By the Middle Ages, the island was in the hands of Clanranald, the Lords of the Isles. Eigg lay at the heart of the Clanranald territory and the island's population found itself embroiled in each of the MacDonald rebellions against the crown and in various clan feuds. In 1566, during a protracted feud between the Macdonalds and the Macleods, a party of MacLeods staying on Eigg took liberties with some local girls. The men were rounded up, bound and cast adrift in the Minch in a small boat and were fortunate to be rescued by some clansmen. Ten years passed before a party of MacLeods from Skye landed on Eigg to exact revenge.

Although already spring, deep snow covered the ground when the Macleods approached Eigg. The island's entire population sought refuge in a secret cave, Uamh Fhraing ('the cave of Francis'). Hidden away along the south coast, the tiny entrance was covered by undergrowth and a small waterfall. After a thorough but fruitless search lasting several days, the MacLeods departed. However, an islander climbed to a vantage point to observe their departure and was spotted. The MacLeods returned and followed his footprints through the snow to the cave. They diverted the stream, and built a fire at the entrance of the cave, filling it with smoke and asphyxiating 395 people inside – the whole population of the island bar one family who managed to escape.

The Massacre Cave sits behind a crevice under a steep rock face. The narrow entrance is less than a metre high and extends for seven metres before opening out. The main chamber of the cave is surprisingly large, at approximately 79m long, 8m wide and 6m high.

In 1588, Eigg – along with the other Small Isles – was sacked by Lachlan Maclean of Duart, who lead a raiding party, including a hundred Spanish marines from a galleon of the defeated Armada lying at Tobermory. The raiders burnt the islands' settlements and murdered many of the islanders, sparing neither women nor children.

The islanders paid a high price for following their clan chiefs during the Jacobite Rebellions of 1715 and 1745. After the failure of the 1745 rebellion, the chief of Clanranald escaped to France, having first taken refuge in a cave at the north end of the island. The islanders who had followed him were captured by the Navy, taken to London and tried. Nineteen of their number died in prison, 18 were transported to Jamaica and only two returned.

Towards the end of the 18th century, the island sustained a population of some 500 people, producing potatoes, oats, black cattle and kelp. The kelp harvesting industry financed construction of the island's main

Galmisdale (photo: James Boulter)

farmhouses, which were tenanted by old Clanranald families, until the clan chiefs' raised rents exponentially, causing many islanders to emigrate to Canada.

In the mid-19th century, the Clearances were visited upon many parts of the Highlands and Islands when sheep farming became very profitable. Higher prices were offered for land empty of people, where sheep could be pastured. On Eigg, the ruined townships of Grulin under the Sgùrr are testament to that bleak period of Highland history. Fourteen families from Grulin were forced to emigrate in 1853.

In 1896 Eigg was bought by Lawrence Thomson, who had made his fortune selling warships to the Japanese. His wealth helped to maintain the estate at a high level and the islanders' lot was generally improved under his stewardship. Thomson died in 1913 and the island passed to his brother before changing hands several times over a short period.

In 1925, the island was purchased by Sir Walter Runciman, a wealthy shipowner and President of the Board of Trade. Lord Runciman built the Lodge and its exotic gardens and used the island as a recreational and sporting estate. Despite not being resident, he initiated an extensive programme of improvements to the island's infrastructure.

During the Second World War, Laig Bay by Cleadale was used by commandos training for the Normandy landings, while many islanders served in the Royal Navy with several seeing action in the Atlantic Convoys. In the post-war world of austerity, economic conditions changed and even though the island was efficiently run as a hill farm it was no longer profitable. The subsequent sale of the island in 1966 was prelude to a long period of instability, with successive owners

who did little to maintain the island community.

After decades of problems with absentee landlords the island was bought in 1997 by the Isle of Eigg Heritage Trust, a partnership between the islanders, the Highland Council and the Scottish Wildlife Trust. The ceremony to mark the handover to community ownership took place on 12 June 1997. A 60 million year old lava pillar standing at the pier commemorates this auspicious day.

WILDLIFE
The largest land mammal on Eigg is the otter, which can be found all around the coastline. Rabbits are abundant. The island wood mouse is said to originate from the Norse settlement, reputedly arriving in Viking longships. Short-tailed voles are very common, long-tailed field mice and pygmy shrews less so. Bats also occur on the island, including a sizeable pipistrelle colony and a few long-eared bats.

Insect life is plentiful and varied; butterflies occur in abundance during the summer months and the island's 18 species include speckled woods, dark green and small pearl bordered fritillaries, and the green hairstreak. In recent years, migrant species have included orange tips, peacock, painted lady and occasional clouded yellows. Nine species of damselfly and dragonfly have been recorded on the island. The friendless midge and cleg – an aggressive horse fly – do occur on Eigg, but in nothing like the numbers suffered on Rum. Toads are present on Eigg, as are common lizards and palmate newts. Adders do not occur.

Both common and grey seals are numerous around the island, particularly on the skerries near the harbour at Galmisdale and Eilean Thuilm at the north end. Minke whales are regularly seen in the waters around the island between July and September. Dolphins of several species and porpoises are common, and killer whales are occasionally spotted. The basking shark is a seasonal visitor, feeding in Eigg's rich coastal waters.

An average of 130 species of bird are recorded annually on Eigg. The island has breeding populations of various raptors: golden eagle, buzzard, peregrine falcon, sparrowhawk, kestrel, hen harrier, barn owl and short and long-eared owls. Eigg has areas of mature woodland and high heather moorland providing habitat for tits, goldcrests, willow-warblers, siskins, flycatchers and bullfinches, among other species. Hooded crows are present in numbers and several pairs of ravens nest on the island. The elusive corncrake has also been recorded in recent years.

Sea birds are less common than on neighbouring islands, and are found mostly at the north end. Puffins, guillemots, razorbills and kittiwakes are seen offshore, while fulmars nest on the south cliffs and Manx shearwaters on the inland cliffs by Cleadale. Cormorants, shags, herring and common gulls, great and lesser black backed gulls are also present.

Red throated and great northern divers, red breasted merganser, eider, shelduck, teal, widgeon, golden eye, oystercatcher, golden and ringed plovers, sanderling, curlew, snipe and sandpiper are among the divers, ducks and waders to be found on Eigg. Passage migrants are numerous, some of which may overwinter, including waxwings, turnstones and bar-tailed godwits, greylag, white-fronted, pink-footed, barnacle and brent geese.

WOODLAND, FLOWERS AND PLANTS

Most of Eigg's central plateau is heather-covered. There is grassland on the lower-lying ground, which is over-run by bracken in some areas. Natural woodland is fairly extensive around Galmisdale, and there are sizeable areas of forestry plantation to the west of the road between Galmisdale and Cleadale. Several exotic species, including eucalyptus, are found in the grounds of Eigg Lodge.

Eigg has been called the 'isle of flowers' by naturalists; its rich and varied plant life includes 500 higher plant species and a bryophyte list numbering well over 300 species, of which over 20 are national rarities. A good deal of the island is covered in hazel scrub woodland, so that bluebells, wild garlic, wood anenome, wood sorrel and primroses abound in spring. Later, in the summer, they are replaced by honeysuckle, enchanter's nightshade and many other species. Twelve species of orchid grow on the island, including the often abundant heath spotted, fragrant and northern marsh orchids. Scarcer species are great butterfly, small white and frog orchids.

The island's cliffs are home to a good cross section of Alpine and Arctic species, particularly on the edges and ledges of the cliffs to the west of Beinn Bhuidhe: cushion pink, globe flowers, mountain avens, both purple and yellow saxifrage, moss campion and the rare arctic

Galmisdale village hall during a music festival (photo: James Boulter)

sandwort. Ferns are abundant and include species such as rusty bark, adderstongue and the odd-looking moonwort.

GETTING AROUND
Visitors are not permitted to bring vehicles to Eigg, and there is no public transport on the island.

Getting around on foot is the norm for most visitors, but bicycles are useful along the island's few kilometres of road. Euan Kirk runs a bike hire service, next to the pierside shops and information centre at Galmisdale, tel: 01687 482405 or 01687 482432.

Davie Robertson operates a minibus taxi service, tel: 01687 482494.

A scheduled minibus service runs between Galmisdale and Cleadale and usually connects with the ferry.

AMENITIES
The exceptionally well-stocked Isle of Eigg Shop is part of the small pierside complex. Opening hours are 10am–5pm Monday–Friday (11am–3pm Thursdays) and between noon and 1pm on Sundays in summer. Orders can be delivered. The Post Office is in the shop and has a cash withdrawal facility, tel: 01687 482432, www.isleofeiggshop.co.uk.

The Galmisdale Bay café, bar and restaurant is situated next to the shop and provides meals and snacks using locally sourced and produced food. Summer opening hours are 9am–10pm Monday–Thursday, 9am–11pm Friday and Saturday and Sunday 11am–5pm. Opening hours are less extensive at other times of year, tel: 01687 482487, www.galmisdale-bay.com.

The Isle of Eigg Craft Shop is also part of the pierside complex and sells local arts and crafts, and pamphlets on Eigg's geology, history and wildlife.

WALK 8

An Sgùrr and Grulin

Start	Galmisdale pier (NM 484 838)
Distance	An Sgùrr return 8km (5 miles); An Sgùrr, Grulin and return 11km (7 miles)
Total Ascent	An Sgùrr return 393m (1290ft); An Sgùrr, Grulin and return 540m (1770ft)
Time	An Sgùrr return 3–3½hrs; An Sgùrr, Grulin and return 4–5hrs
Map	OS Explorer 397: OS Landranger 39

An unsurpassed vantage point for magnificent views of Rum, Coll, Muck, the Outer Hebrides, Skye, the Ardnamurchan peninsula and the mainland mountains of Lochaber, the instantly recognisable towering pitchstone monolith of An Sgùrr is visible far and wide.

Climbing An Sgùrr from Galmisdale makes for a fine half-day walk – a good leg-stretcher, though not especially challenging. However, walking along the summit ridge provides a stimulatingly exposed sensation as the world literally drops away on three sheer cliff-faced sides at the actual summit. The route is mostly waymarked and not difficult to follow; the ground can be boggy in places once the track from Galmisdale is left behind. Continuing on to the ruins of the cleared villages of Grulin from An Sgùrr makes for a very worthwhile extension to this route, though some navigation is required as the vague paths are difficult to follow and the terrain is awkward in places.

From Galmisdale pier, follow the left-hand track/road, which climbs gently north-west and soon enters woodland. Keep straight on (left) where the track forks after 500 metres, following red waymarkers. ◄

The right fork leads to the village hall.

A little further on, a left-hand turn leads ultimately to the Massacre Cave (a worthwhile detour on the return); keep straight on, climbing steadily before emerging from the woods through a gate – An Sgùrr now dominating the horizon.

Follow the track up across the field towards a house and pass through a gate to its right-hand side. Turn left onto a track and after 80 metres join the waymarked path climbing away from the track on the right-hand side at NM 474 841. This

The path passes under the towering north flank of An Sgùrr

Lochan beneath An Sgùrr

well-trodden path climbs steadily all the way to the summit of An Sgùrr and is mostly easy to follow, but it traverses heather-covered peaty terrain, which is boggy in places.

The path climbs past the impressive sheer cliff forming **An Sgùrr**'s eastern face before traversing beneath the northern flank of the summit ridge as the gradient slackens. The path soon turns south and climbs steeply up through a gully to a narrow grassy saddle across the spine of the ridge. ◄

From here there are great views onto the isle of Muck.

Follow the red paint waymarkers east (left) up onto the exposed rock of the summit ridge and continue for 500 metres to reach the summit, which is marked by a 'Vanessa' triangulation pillar. On a clear day the views are stunning and the sheer drop on three sides makes for an airy sensation.

Descend by the same route. To return to Galmisdale, simply retrace your outward steps.

Continuation to Grulin

To continue on to Grulin, descend as far as the foot of the northern flank of the summit ridge beneath the gully. From here, look for a faint trodden path heading west north-west. Follow this to the south-eastern end of **Loch**

nam Ban Mòra, across heathery, boggy ground. Skirt the south-western shore of the loch on a vague path that climbs a short way from the loch edge at one point. At the western extremity of the loch turn south-west (you may be able to follow a vague path) and head over a rise to arrive above the north-western end of a beautiful lochan tucked beneath the Sgùrr. Head north-west for 300 metres on a faint path to skirt around the north end of another fine lochan; continue north-west a short way from the lochan before beginning to descend.

The descent from here to the Grulin path can be awkward as there is dense heather cover to negotiate and steep rocky outcrops to avoid, but it involves no real hazard. Pick a good line of descent from above and make a gradual traverse rather than dropping directly – the ruins of Grulin should soon be visible below. At the foot of the slope follow a distinct path that leads south-east.

> Take time to explore the ruins of the abandoned villages of **Grulin**, which are perched above the coast with a fine outlook on to the isle of Muck.

From Grulin, follow the path – which soon becomes a track – contouring along beneath An Sgùrr, with fine views of its sheer south face. The track is easy to follow and passes the turn-off for the path to An Sgùrr after 3.3km: 80 metres further on, turn right through a gate and retrace your outward route back to Galmisdale.

WALK 9

Around the coast and cliffs of north Eigg

Start	Galmisdale (NM 484 838); Cleadale to Galmisdale along the coast: Cleadale (NM 477 886)
Distance	26km (16 miles); clifftop only route: 16.5km (10½ miles); Cleadale to Galmisdale along the coast: 14km (8.5 miles)
Total Ascent	995m (3265ft); clifftop only route: 631m (2070ft); Cleadale to Galmisdale along the coast: 457m (1500ft)
Time	8–9hrs; clifftop only route: 5–6hrs; Cleadale to Galmisdale along the coast: 4–5hrs
Map	OS Explorer 397: OS Landranger 39

Tackling this route in its entirety makes for a tough day's walk, but an unusual and rewarding hike of two halves where the terrain changes significantly and the same views are enjoyed from different perspectives. Walking the coast route and the cliff top route separately makes for two good half-day walks. The cliff top route around the Beinn Bhuidhe plateau can be very rough in places, especially on the eastern side; sinuous, calf-length heather and boggy ground make for tough going, but a trodden path aids progress significantly. The cliff top along the western side benefits from soft, springy turf for much of its length. The views are spectacular on all sides in clear conditions. A route back to the start is described below for those wanting to walk just the hilltop route.

The coast walk, which can be done by itself, starts amid the scattered settlement of Cleadale, which looks out across the Sound of Rum to that island's jagged Cuillin hills. A towering arc of black basalt cliffs rises in a vertical wall to the rear of Cleadale; the route passes beneath them, then around the island's northern extremity before continuing south along the shore of Eigg's east coast beneath the impressive cliffs forming the eastern flank of the Beinn Bhuidhe plateau. The going can be rough and awkward in places along the east coast, but gives no real difficulties in reasonable conditions.

> From Galmisdale pier, follow the road around the bay for 450 metres, turning right off the road to follow a track (orange waymarkers) continuing around the bay. Cross

Cleadale, with the basalt cliffs forming the western flank of the Beinn Bhuidhe plateau

a burn flowing out to the shore via stepping stones. Head across the greensward and go through a metal gate (orange waymarker). Turn right to follow a track up a rise then descend to cross a stile (orange waymarker). Continue along the path, turn left at a small wooden sign and follow the winding path downhill through shrubbery, passing through a gate. Continue along the path, go through another gate then turn left onto a road just above **Poll nam Partan**. Continue along the road for 250 metres, turn right onto a track road, passing a house after 250 metres. Cross a burn, turn left onto a track and continue north-east, soon passing through a stock gate in a dry stone wall. Continue for 350 metres along the track and go through another stock gate.

Continue north along the track for just over 1km to arrive by a dry stone walled sheepfold. Continue past the sheepfold, go through a gate and head north across rough, often boggy terrain with thick heather cover. Go through another gate and continue along the cliff tops following a flattened path through the dense heather cover. This path stays close to the cliff tops for much of the way to the north-western extremity of Dùn Thalasgair but it does trend inland a little around Sgorr Gobhar to the east of the summit of **An Cruachan**.

Eilean Thuilm

Sgorr
Sgaileach

T a l m

Dùnan
Thalasgeir

Boghana
Brice nis

Blàr Mòr

336

Coire
na Falain

50

Camas
Sgiotaig

T o l a i n

Srón na
h-Iolaire

Cleadale

SF

Sgorr an
Fharaidh

B e i n n   B h u i d h e

89

Waterfall

Rubha nan Trì Chlach

49

A' Chuagach

Waterfalls

S r u t h

Waterfall

88

Bealach
Clìth

Waterfalls

299
An Cruachan

SF

Waterfall

Blàr Dubh

Monadh a' Bhràighe

EIGG

87

P Mus

School

B l à r   M ò r

Glac an
Dorchadais

Standing
Stone

Bealach
Clìth

Leac
a' Ghuidhal

41
Crois
Mhòr

Kildonan

mhor

Rubha na
Crannáig

nam Partan

Flod Sgeir

Piers

Garbh Sgeir

Meml
Galmisdale

Continue north, crossing the occasional burn and be sure to take in the view where the Allt na h-Airde Mheadhonaich tumbles over the cliff edge. A kilometre further on, by **Sròn na h-Iolaire**, leave the cliff edge as it begins to lose height – keep your height and contour along trending north-west. There are vague paths to aid your progress and the heather cover is less dense. Cross the Allt Ceann a' Gharaid, which flows out from Loch na Beinne Bhuidhe, continue north-west and you will soon arrive at the cliff edge once more. Follow the cliff top north-west, soon arriving at **Dùnan Thalasgair**. Turn south-west to follow a fence for 150 metres to a gate, go through and follow the path outside the fence along the cliff tops for a short way. ▶

The views of Rum are spectacular on a clear day.

Turn around the end of the fence and continue along the narrow but distinct path along the cliff tops, soon passing over the summit of **Beinn Bhuidhe** (336m), which is marked with a 'Vanessa' triangulation pillar.

Continue along the soft, springy turf on the cliff top path, passing over the high point of **Sgorr an Fhàraidh** after a further 1km. The path begins to descend steadily along the cliff edge and arrives above the impressive waterfall of the Allt Bidein an Tighearna after another 1km. Cross the burn to enjoy the view from behind the rock pinnacle known as Bidein an Tighearna – 'God's Finger' – down across Cleadale and the Bay of Laig.

Looking down the waterfall of the Allt na h-Airde Mheadonaich from the Beinn Bhuide plateau

Return to Galmisdale via An Cruachan

From Bidein an Tighearna, head south-east following the burn for about 300 metres. Turn south, climb a little crossing an old drystone wall and continue a short way to the summit of **An Cruachan** (299m). The summit is featureless and the small summit cairn can be hard to find. From the summit, continue a short way south-east then trend south-south-east descending gradually along the

On the summit of An Cruachan, looking towards Rum (photo: Peter Khambatta)

ridge, crossing a fence and a wall, avoiding the rough heather-cover where possible. Make for the dry stone walled sheepfold near the eastern edge of the plateau, passing through a stock gate. Retrace the outward route to return to **Galmisdale**.

Continue descending along the cliff tops on the obvious path. Cross a stock fence by a step stile and continue descending steadily following a vague path. The path passes through an overgrown copse of small trees and shrubs, crosses a burn, then continues downhill to arrive at the road next to a disused quarry. Turn right and follow the road down hill to **Cleadale**.

Take the left-hand fork in the road by the Lageòrna restaurant (NM 477 886) and follow the road for around 600 metres until it peters out by a house and some farm buildings. Following blue waymarkers, continue on the obvious path that swings left to the rear of the house and continues across fields to the edge of low cliffs. Continue north along the cliff edge inside a stock fence and then cross a stile to descend to the beach.

As well as the 'singing sands' of Tràigh a' Bhìgeil, the shore fringing **Camas Sgiotaig** is home to some weird and wonderful weather sculpted sandstone rock formations and is worth exploring.

Walk along to the north end of the beach and cross rocks and pebbles to continue around the coast just above the shore on a narrow trodden path, which is a little awkward to follow in places. After 2km you will arrive by the dry stone walled enclosure at **Talm**. ▶

Seals can usually be seen basking on Eilean Thuilm a few hundred metres offshore.

Alternative route from Cleadale to Talm

This route is 1km shorter than the route via Tràigh a' Bhìgeil. Where the road through Cleadale forks just north of the Lageòrna restaurant (NM 477 886), take the right-hand fork and continue along the road, passing the settlement's scattering of houses. The road becomes a track as it passes through Howlin. The track passes some farm buildings and becomes a path – prone to bogginess – which soon climbs steadily up and over 'The Saddle' (150m), crossing a stock fence by a step stile.

The path is initially distinct as it descends steeply beneath the north-west flank of the cliffs immediately below **Dùnan Thalasgair**. Where the path levels amid a terrain of scattered rocks, follow it around to the north-east, making for a broad gully. Cross to the eastern side of the gully and follow it down to the shore next to an old dry stone walled enclosure at **Talm**.

Continue initially east following a narrow path to the landward side of the low cliff at **Sgorr Sgaileach**. Climb a little over Fhaing Ruadh and then descend to the shore following a small gully a short way before skirting around to the left to find the easiest line down to the pebble beach. ▶

High above, the impressive waterfall of the Allt Ceann a' Gharaid drops precipitously over the towering cliff edge.

Walk a short way along the edge of the pebble beach and then continue along a narrow path. Stay with this path for 5km or so to arrive at the **Bealach Clìth**, where the coast is left behind. The path is generally easy to follow and stays just above the shore for the most part until the last kilometre or so, where it climbs as the gradient between the shore and the foot of the cliffs steepens. The path becomes much more distinct at this point and is even marked on the 1:25,000 OS map. The going can be awkward at times with some rough ground and rocks to negotiate in places. The views along the towering basalt cliffs of the east coast and across the sound to Sleat, Morar and Arisaig are compensation for any hardship.

Follow the path up through the gap in the cliffs by the Bealach Clìth, climbing to a metal gate. Go through and continue south-west parallel to a dry stone wall for 250 metres to arrive at a track and turn left through the gateway. Retrace the outward route to return to **Galmisdale**. If you've omitted the cliff walk section and have just walked the coast from Cleadale you might appreciate the following directions.

Return route to Galmisdale

Continue along the track heading south past the sheepfold, descending steadily and passing through a gate in a drystone wall after 1km. Continue along the track, passing through a gate in another dry stone wall after 350 metres. Continue along the track a short way then turn right, cross a burn and pass a house next to some woodland. Join a track road and follow it for 250 metres to arrive at a road. Turn left onto the road and follow it down towards the shore at **Poll nam Partan**. Turn right onto a footpath through shrubbery above the beach and go through a gate with an orange waymark. Continue through another gate; the path leaves the shrubbery and winds uphill; follow a small wooden sign pointing right rather than following the footpath continuing straight on. Cross a stile (orange waymark) and follow the left-hand path to the top of the rise before descending to arrive at a track road. Turn left along the track, go through a metal gate (orange waymark) and continue across the greensward to cross a burn flowing out to the shore via stepping stones. Continue along the footpath leading to the road. Turn left onto the road to continue for 450 metres to **Galmisdale**.

CANNA
Canaigh; Eilean Chanaigh

Along the cliffs on Canna's north coast (Walk 10)

INTRODUCTION

The ancient turret atop Coroghon Mòr once imprisoned a witch

Canna is the westernmost and the second smallest of the Small Isles archipelago. It is linked to its tide-separated sister, Sanday, by a bridge and by sandbanks and a road at low tide. Canna is approximately 8km (5 miles) long and 1.5km (1 mile) wide. Sanday is about 1.5km (1 mile) long and 0.5km wide.

Canna is mainly comprised of two plateaus 50–200m above sea level, which are joined by a low-lying isthmus at Tarbert. There are towering basalt cliffs along most of the north coast and the island's highest point is Carn a' Ghaill (210m) above the cliffs at the north-east. Canna's coastline, with its often spectacular cliffs, geological features and ancient monuments, provides the focus for walkers,

and the entire island can be walked round in a long day. Sanday is easily strolled around in a few hours and is well worth a visit to watch the puffins nesting on the sea stacks of Dùn

Mòr and Dùn Beag from April to July. In fine weather the views over to the north-west of Rum are reason enough to visit Sanday.

There is a large natural harbour between Canna and Sanday and the pier was rebuilt and enlarged in 2005. This is used by the CalMac ferry, MV Lochnevis, which connects Canna and the neighbouring Small Isles with the mainland port of Mallaig. National Trust for Scotland (NTS) permission is required to land motor vehicles on the island. The sheltered harbour is the only deep water harbour in the Small Isles and attracts considerable yachting traffic.

In 1981, Canna and Sanday were given to the NTS by their previous owner, the Gaelic folklorist and scholar John Lorne Campbell. Since then, the NTS has tried to attract new residents and visitors to the islands. The islands are primarily run as a farm and conservation area, with some crofting on Sanday.

A'Chill, situated at the head of the natural harbour, was Canna's main settlement until the island was cleared in 1851. The post-clearance population of Canna and Sanday was recorded as 119 in 1881. The population continued to decline, stabilising at around 20 to 30 during the second half of the 20th century. By the 2001 census, however, the number had dwindled to 12. Since then, new residents have settled on the island, bringing the 2011 population of Canna and Sanday to around 21. There are no roads and no shops other than a Post Office.

GEOLOGY

Canna and Sanday are largely composed of lavas erupted during the Lower Tertiary period from a major volcano on what would become the Isle of Skye. While the volcano was erupting, the area was traversed by fast-flowing rivers which deposited thick layers of boulder conglomerate. These boulders were rounded as they were carried along in the immensely powerful rapid flowing currents – the largest are over a metre in diameter.

Canna is also noted for the tiers of basalt pillars rising over the eastern half of the island and the sea cliffs that dominate its northern shore. On the eastern edge of the island, Compass Hill (139m) is formed of volcanic rock known as tuff, which is of such high iron content that passing ships' compasses are distorted, pointing east, rather than north. Raised shore platforms occur, notably beneath the cliffs at the island's west. Along the coastline near the south-eastern extremity of Sanday stand two impressive sea stacks, Dùn Mòr and Dùn Beag, which are formed of columnar basalt lavas and boulder conglomerate.

HISTORY

Canna has been inhabited for at least 5000 years. Extensive finds of Neolithic pottery have been made at Tarbert, the low-lying isthmus between Canna's two plateaus. A fortification known as Dùn Channa, possibly dating to the Bronze Age, sits atop a rock stack at the island's western extremity. During its late prehistory, around AD600, Canna was likely occupied by a mixture of Celtic and pre-Celtic peoples generally described as Picts.

The earliest historical references relate to the patron saint of the island, Saint Columba (AD597–521), after whom two of the churches are named. There are traces of two early Christian sites on the island, at Keill, where a stone cross dates from the eighth century, and at Sgorr nam Bàn Naomh (cliff of the holy women), a walled enclosure situated on a raised shore platform below steep cliffs that is thought to have been a nunnery.

Like the rest of the Hebrides, Canna was affected by Viking raids and subsequent settlement from the ninth century. The Norse influence is evident in the place-names 'Sanday' and 'Tarbert' and also the site known as Uamh Rìgh Lochlainn, the Cave of the Norse King, which is believed to be a burial site, although there is no archaeological evidence to support this. If monastic life on Canna was disrupted by Viking raids, it had resumed by the Middle Ages and continued until at least the 15th century with the island remaining the property of Iona Abbey until 1627.

With the end of Norse rule in the 12th century, Canna became part of the territory of Clanranald – the Lords of the Isles. Under Clanranald rule, the island's population found itself involved in the MacDonald clan's feuds and rebellions against the crown. In 1588, Canna – along with the other Small Isles – was laid waste by Lachlan Maclean of Duart leading a raiding party of a hundred Spanish marines from a galleon of the defeated

Saint Columba's Presbyterian church, known locally as the Rocket Church

Canna House

Armada anchored at Tobermory. The islands' settlements were razed and its inhabitants murdered.

The Clanranald chiefs were among the staunchest supporters of the Stuart cause during the Civil Wars and Canna men were among those enlisted with Bonnie Prince Charlie's forces during the Jacobite Rebellion of 1745. In the wake of the failed rebellion, harsh reprisals were visited on the islanders by government troops.

The failure of the rising undermined Clanranald's fortunes; by the early 19th century it was deeply in debt and obliged to sell most of its territories, including Canna. The island was made to pay at the point when its population had peaked at over 400. A series of clearances saw most of the population moved to poorer land on Sanday. The situation was worsened by crop failures and the decline of the kelp farming industry. Thus began a process of depopulation, which continued into the 20th century.

Canna was bought by Dr John Lorne Campbell, the eminent Gaelic scholar and author, in 1938. He widened the pier, improved the soil, increased the amount of woodland and modernised the cottages of his crofting tenants. He also farmed the land himself, rearing sheep and cattle. Campbell and his wife, the American musician Margaret Fay Shaw, travelled throughout the Hebrides collecting Gaelic folklore and songs: their archive is kept at Canna House, their former home, and was given to the NTS along with the islands.

Today the island is managed by the NTS as a single livestock farm. Conservation of the island's landscape, monuments and habitats, together with the encouragement of rare species – including the corncrake and white-tailed eagle – are high on the agenda. Sanday is still crofted by some of its inhabitants.

WILDLIFE

There are no large land mammals on Canna, but there are otters. By 2005 the island's brown rat population had grown to 10,000, posing such a threat to nesting birds, including the rare Manx shearwater, that a complete cull was necessary. As rodenticide was used, a breeding population of the island's distinct race of woodmice, *Apodemus sylvaticus*, was removed

beforehand. By the end of 2006 Canna was declared rat-free. The mice were returned and are thriving. However, since the eradication of the rats the rabbit population has grown exponentially. White-tailed eagles, golden eagles and buzzards will take rabbits, but they have their work cut out. Hedgehogs were introduced in 1938.

Canna is renowned for its birdlife, including white-tailed eagles, golden eagles, peregrine falcons, buzzards, hooded crows, ravens and the elusive corncrake. Sea birds breeding on the island include puffins, guillemots, kittiwakes, fulmars and the great skua or 'bonxie'. Predation by rats seriously affected Canna's seabird colonies, particularly razorbills, shags and Manx shearwaters, but these are recovering well since the rat eradication programme. In the

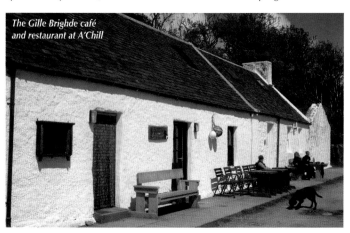

The Gille Brighde café and restaurant at A'Chill

waters around Canna and Sanday, Atlantic grey and common seals, dolphins, porpoises, minke whales and basking sharks can be seen.

There are some 260 varieties of butterflies and moths, many of them unique to the island. Butterfly species include green hairstreak, speckled wood, grayling, small pearl-bordered fritillary and dark green fritillary. Moths include death's head hawkmoth, sallow kitten, yellow horned, pale oak eggar, white ermine, dew moth, nut-tree tussock, large emerald, transparent burnet, ghost moth and bee moth.

TREES, FLOWERS AND PLANTS
There is little indigenous woodland on Canna – a few specimens of rowan, hazel, aspen, sallow and creeping willow are all that remain. Much of the native tree cover was likely felled for firewood when the island was more populous, and the introduction of sheep and rabbits inhibited regeneration. A number of species have been introduced – mostly since 1881 – including sycamore, wych elm, cherry, hawthorn, ash, elder, lime, whitebeam and Serbian spruce. Exotics include Antarctic beech, southern beech and dawn redwood.

The island's mild, Gulf Stream-assisted climate, fertile soil and sheltered position have earned Canna the name 'garden of the Hebrides'. Farming is an important part of Canna's economy, and the island supports livestock grazing and arable feed crops. Among the island's many plant species, bell heather, lady fern and various grasses, sedges, rushes, thistles and umbellifers thrive amid the varied terrain. Sea pinks grow along the shore, daffodils proliferate in March and April, bluebells and flag iris abound in spring and primroses can be found almost year-round. Canna has several varieties of orchid: marsh spotted, heath spotted, early purple, frog and the rare greater butterfly orchid.

GETTING AROUND
Visitors are only permitted to bring vehicles to Canna and Sanday with NTS authorisation: there is no public transport on the islands and just a few kilometres of track road. Getting around on foot or bike are the only options.

AMENITIES
There are no shops on Canna, so bring your own supplies. The Post Office is a converted garden shed. Gille Brighde, the island's licensed café and restaurant, provides light lunches, soups, snacks and homebaking during the day and a rustic style menu in the evenings, using fresh seafood and local meat including wild rabbit. Closed Sunday evenings and Monday, tel: 01687 460164, www. cannarestaurant.com. There is currently no mobile phone coverage but there is a working red telephone box and satellite internet access.

WALK 10

Around the coast of Canna

Start	A'Chill (NG 272 053)
Distance	20km (12½ miles)
Total Ascent	750m (2460ft)
Time	7–8½hrs
Map	OS Explorer 397: OS Landranger 39

This fine circular route around Canna's magnificent coastline is exposed to the elements for much of its course along the island's dramatic high cliffs and provides fantastic views of Skye, Rum, Barra and South Uist on a clear day. Several sites of historical interest lie close to the route and the high point of Carn a' Ghaill (210m) is close to the cliff top path. The terrain is not especially tough – though the ground can be boggy; the heather cover is kept short by the wind and a narrow path can be followed along much of the cliff tops. There is a track running along the raised shore platform between Tarbert and A'Chill. The entire route makes for a demanding day's walk – alternatively it can be split into two parts.

From the small, scattered settlement of A'Chill, walk north-east along the track road, taking the left-hand fork along a track where the road bears south-east towards the pier. Continue along the track towards the rock stack of Coroghon Mòr, with its crumbling stone turret. Before reaching Coroghon Mòr, however, pass to the rear (left) of an old stone building, go through a stock gate on the left, continue north across the field and climb a slope towards the eastern end of a woodland plantation. Go through a gate and climb north then north-east to the summit of **Compass Hill** (139m), the high point at Canna's eastern end.

Along the cliffs on Canna's north coast (Walk 10)

Compass Hill is formed of a volcanic rock known as tuff, which has such a high iron content that passing ships' compasses are distorted, pointing east rather than north.

The views from Compass Hill on a clear day are truly wonderful – to the north and north-east the isle of Skye dominates the horizon, and the view south-east across Sanday to the western hills of Rum is magnificent.

Map continues on page 121

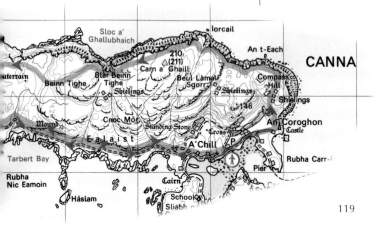

119

From the summit of Compass Hill head towards the cliff tops on the north coast then continue west following a narrow path close to the cliff edge – there are sections of stock fence along the cliff tops at strategic points. Cross a stock fence via a step stile, continue along the narrow cliff top path through the low heather cover to arrive at a section of cliff top fence with a stile crossing to the cliff tops after 600 metres. Don't cross here but continue inside the fence, descending a short way to cross a burn at an obvious point. Continue along the cliff top – keeping a lookout for white-tailed eagles – and soon cross the 200m contour on the cliffward side of **Carn a'Ghaill** (210m); a 150 metre detour to the south takes you to Canna's highest point, marked with a 'Vanessa' triangulation pillar.

Continue along the narrow cliff top path, losing a little height. Stay on the inside of the stock fence where twin gullies tumble precipitously down to the shore at **Sloc a' Ghallubhaich** – there is a dramatic view northwest along the sea cliffs beneath Beinn Tighe. Walk on, climbing a short way to cross a fence by a step stile, then continue up and over the seaward flank of **Beinn Tighe**. Cross another fence, continue contouring south-west a short way along the flank of the hill before dropping into and descending south-west along a broad gully, which is boggy in places. Descend to a dry stone wall and follow this north then north-west. Where the wall turns south again continue west across country for about 400 metres to arrive atop low cliffs. Continue south along the cliff edge before crossing a fence on a step stile then descending towards a gate in a dry stone wall. To visit the bay at **Camas Thairbearnais**, turn right and head for the shore.

Shorter variant

To return directly to A'Chill, turn left and go through a gate in the dry stone wall running at right angles to the wall you've just passed through. Follow a track south-south-east across a large enclosed field for 400 metres to arrive at a gate at the south end of the field. Go through and turn left to join the track that soon climbs a short way then descends before running along the raised shore platform beneath the southern cliffs for 4km back to **A'Chill**.

To continue along the full route, head south-west across the field to a gate at a wall and a stock fence junction (NG 237 058). Go through the gate and turn right, continuing initially north-west across boggy ground to regain the cliff tops. Continue along the cliff top path, soon turning south along a stock fence above the **Allt na Crìche Tuatha**. Cross the fence by a step stile, cross the burn and continue along the cliff top path. Cross a burn after 450 metres and on arriving at another burn after 1.2km (NG 216 056), descend a distinct path to the raised shore platform beneath the cliffs.

> It is well worth abandoning the cliff tops to explore this **undercliff domain**; the remains of sheilings, walled enclosures and the corrugations of ancient lazy beds are testament to the struggle of Canna's earlier inhabitants to eke a living from the land. A dazzling outcrop of white shell sand makes a perfect spot to sit and admire the fine views back along the cliffs to the east.

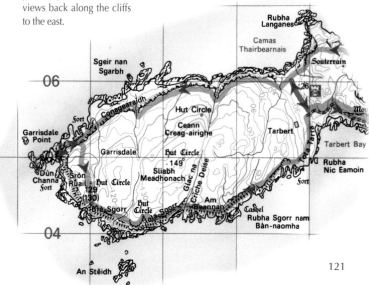

It is both possible and worthwhile to continue along the shore platform as far as **Garrisdale Point**.

This is a **dramatic coastal landscape**, not far above sea level, and the views from Garrisdale Point are impressive. A short way to the south, standing clear of the cliffs, is the once-fortified rock stack of Dùn Channa. The lighthouse on the islet of Hyskeir – or Òigh-sgeir – is visible 10km to the south-west.

From Garrisdale Point retrace your steps north-east for 250 metres and climb back to the cliff tops by way of the obvious grassy slopes. Continue climbing gently south to arrive at the high-cliff summit of **Sròn Ruail** (129m), with its commanding views over the Sea of the Hebrides and along Canna's southern cliffs.

Continue initially south-east along the cliff tops – the going is generally easier along the southern cliffs with less heather, although the ground can be boggy in places. Descend a short way to cross a burn on a pair of wooden

Looking down on the raised shore platform beneath Canna's northern cliffs

beams and continue along the cliff top path, gaining and losing a little height along the way and crossing the occasional burn as the view over to Rum's north-western hills opens up magnificently.

Around 1.8km beyond Sròn Ruail, cross a burn, go through a stock gate and climb to the dramatic cliff top summit of **Am Beannan**.

Walking along Canna's southern cliffs with north-west Rum on the horizon

> To the east of Am Beannan on the raised shore platform beneath Sgorr nam Bàn Naomh ('cliff of the holy women') are the **remains of a walled enclosure** that is thought to have been an early-Christian monastic hermitage – possibly a nunnery, hence the name. A fixed rope aids access to the shore platform, but a descent should only be attempted in good conditions, with due caution by one person at a time.

From Am Beannan continue north-east along the cliff tops, descend a short way, cross a burn and continue for around 500 metres across a stretch of boggy ground before arriving at a stock fence. Go through the gate and descend gently, following the grass track sweeping around to the north above the coastline as it cuts in to Canna's wasp waist at

123

Tarbert Bay. Contour along above Tota Tarra, making for the track to the north-east of a long stone building.

Join the track, which soon climbs a short way before descending to the raised shore platform again and continuing on its winding way for 4km back to **A'Chill**. ◄

There is plenty to enjoy along the route with great views across Sanday to Rum and activity from sea birds, waders and divers. With luck or forethought, you'll arrive when the lovely Gille Brighde café and restaurant is open to enjoy a reviving beverage.

This last section
is a relatively
undemanding final
chapter to a big day's
walk.

Shorter alternative
To walk just the western half of Canna's coastline, follow the track road west from A'Chill to Tarbert. At the end of the track, turn right through a gate in a dry stone walled enclosure, cross the enclosure following the grassy track to its northernmost extremity, go through a gate, turn left along the dry stone wall, cross a burn and arrive at a gate at the junction between the wall and a stock fence. Go through the gate and follow the main route description from NG 237 058.

WALK 11
Around Sanday

Start	Bridge linking Canna and Sanday (NG 266 050)
Distance	11km (7 miles)
Total Ascent	236m (755ft)
Time	3–3½hrs
Map	OS Explorer 397: OS Landranger 39

After the demanding day-long walk along Canna's towering cliffs, Sanday provides the perfect opportunity to take things easier with a half-day ramble around its gentle, low-lying coast. In fact, a walk around Sanday is the perfect diversion while awaiting an afternoon ferry to Mallaig or one of the other Small Isles.

Chief among Sanday's attractions are the impressive rock stacks of Dùn Mòr and Dùn Beag, which are alive with nesting sea birds – including puffins – from late spring. The views across the Sound of Canna to Bloodstone Hill, Orval and Fionchra on Rum are worth the visit to Sanday alone.

Cross the bridge linking the tide-separated islands and turn right, passing a Marian shrine with a stained-glass Madonna and child. After 100 metres go through a wooden gate next to a stock gate, cross a small, beautiful sandy beach and make for a wooden stock gate above its south-western end. Go through the gate and follow the coastline as it turns south, crossing boggy ground, before gaining the cliffs climbing to Sanday's highest point at **Tallabric** (59m). ▸

Descend east along the cliff top inside the stock fence. Arriving above a bay, follow the stock fence inland for 150 metres and go through a wooden stock gate. Continue around the low-lying coastline on the soft, springy turf, then skirt around the seaward flank of Cnoc Ghreannabric along low cliffs, with excellent views across the bay at **Sùileabhaig**, with the easternmost part of Sanday and Rum beyond. Descend along the cliffs and

This clifftop vantage point provides fine views across Sanday and Canna's southern cliffs as well as onto Rum, Muck, Ardnamurchan, Coll and Tiree.

Looking back to Canna and the footbridge linking Canna and Sanday from north-west Sanday

go through a gate in a stock fence. Continue around the bay, skirting above the pebble beach and passing through a collapsed dry stone wall. Turn sharply north-east along a low cliff top then follow a dry stone wall along to a gate. Go through the gate, follow the track straight ahead a short way before turning south to pass a lochan and small reed marsh. The ground in this area is often boggy and churned up by cattle – there are some stepping stones across the outflow of the lochan.

Climb to the cliff tops once again, soon looking on to the rock stacks of **Dùn Mòr** and Dùn Beag. Continue along the cliff top, descending then climbing a little to arrive at a vantage point with the best views of the rock stacks.

Puffins can be seen here during the nesting season with the aid of binoculars. Puffins nest in deep burrows or crevices so are seen either around the stacks or floating in 'rafts' of dozens of birds in the surrounding sea.

From the viewpoint, descend directly north then cross above the head of an inlet, which frames a dramatic view of Dùn Beag, and continue around the headland on a narrow path a short way back from the coast. Turn north and pass to landward of the lighthouse: continue contouring around the headland as the coastline turns west again. Continue above Camas Stianabhaig – the ground can be boggy in places – and make directly for the gate in the dry stone wall cutting across the neck of the headland. Go through the gate and continue straight ahead (northwest) making for the landmark of St Edward's church. Go through a stock gate and head for the dry stone wall to the east of the church; follow the wall along to a gate and go through to arrive by the **St Edwards Centre**.

The deconsecrated Saint Edward's church, Sanday

127

Standing alone on an elevated part of the island, the deconsecrated **Catholic church of St Edward** is the largest and most conspicuous building on Sanday. The church now belongs to the Hebridean Trust, which converted it into a hostel and study centre linked to the archive of Gaelic culture and folklore created by the late John Lorne Campbell, the former owner of Canna and Sanday. The centre was officially opened in 2001, but has remained locked and unused since then.

When the tide is very high you may have to continue along the inside of the stock fence.

Follow the obvious track north-west down towards the shore, go through a stock gate and follow the track skirting south-west along the shoreline. ◀

Stained glass detail from a Marian shrine by the Sanday–Canna footbridge

Follow the track around to the school and small collection of houses and, unless the tide is very high, continue along the track skirting around the shore until you arrive back at the bridge once more. If the tide is very high, follow the track heading initially south-west between the houses and the school and follow it as it trends west then north and leads to the bridge.

MUCK
Eilean nam Muc

Port Mòr on Muck (Walk 12)

INTRODUCTION

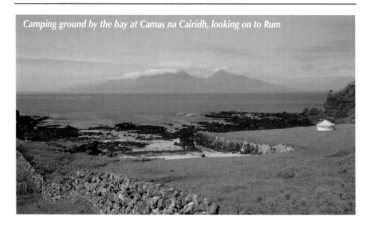

Camping ground by the bay at Camas na Cairidh, looking on to Rum

Muck is the smallest and most fertile of the Small Isles, measuring approximately 4km (2½ miles) east to west and 2.5km (1½ miles) north to south at its widest point. It lies 4km (2½ miles) south-west of Eigg and is 13km north of Ardnamurchan, the western-most point on the mainland of Britain. The lowest-lying of the Small Isles, its high point is Beinn Airein (137m).

Muck has been owned by the MacEwen family since 1896 and most of the island is run as a single livestock farm. The population of 30 mostly lives near the harbour at Port Mòr. The other settlement on the island is the farm at Gallanach. The island's only road, which is about 2.5km (1½ miles) long, connects the two. Port Mòr House is the island's only hotel. Muck is also known for its

seal population, and for the porpoises in the surrounding waters. In fact, the name may derive from the Gaelic word for porpoise, *muc mara* – literally, 'sea pig'.

Owing to its small size, Muck can be walked around in its entirety in a good half day or so. The route in this guidebook starts at Port Mòr and heads anti-clockwise around the coast, taking in the headland of Am Maol, Gallanach Bay, Beinn Airein, Camas Mòr and Caisteal an Dùin Bhàin before returning to Port Mòr. If the tide is low it is also possible to walk across to the outlying islets of Eilean Ard nan Uan and Eilean nan Each from the Ard nan Uan promontory – Muck's northernmost point.

When the weather is clement there can be few British islands as idyllic as Muck. Even when the ferry has delivered a batch of visitors outnumbering the island's population, Muck's tranquil air remains little disturbed. In high winds, however, the picture can be very different as the low-lying island is exposed to the full fury of storms blowing in off the Atlantic. However, Muck's low profile also allows for some tremendous views across to the mountainous aspects of Rum and Eigg as well as the mainland coast.

GEOLOGY

Muck is largely composed of basalt lava flows originating from Tertiary Age volcanic centres on Ardnamurchan and Rum. These lava flows are clearly visible in step-like features comprising small escarpments formed from the hard, slow-cooling core of each flow, with gentler slopes between composed of the softer, more easily eroded rock formed above and below the core.

High cliffs of western Muck (Walk 12)

Rugged inlet at Sloc na Dubhaich (Walk 12)

Beneath the basalts are a series of sandstones, limestones and shales formed during the Jurassic Period. On Muck, these are exposed on the shore at Camus Mòr. Doleritic basalt dikes are common on Muck; these were formed by upwelling magma filling fissures in the Earth's crust radiating out from centres of volcanic eruption. Erosion of the less-resistant rock they are intruded into has left them exposed as natural walls, giving rise to the broken coastline of Muck. There is also a large gabbro dike on the east side of Fang Mòr.

The processes of glaciation removed much of the pre-glacial soils from the island. However, these have been replaced by loam soils produced by rapid weathering of the country rock combined with wind-blown sand.

HISTORY

Burial cairns at Ard nan Uan on the west side of Gallanach date from the Neolithic or early Bronze Age (about 2000bc). On the peninsula south-west of Port Mòr, overlooking the harbour entrance, a Bronze Age fortification known as Caisteal an Dùin Bhàin ('Castle of the White Fort') sits atop a volcanic bluff – a cylindrical upthrust of rock with vertical cliffs 6m high all round. The structure incorporates a perimeter wall, two staggered gateways and internal walls.

Muck was likely settled by the Norsemen. There are many Norse place names throughout the Small Isles – including the hills of Rum and the valleys of Eigg – but in Muck only the names Taolun and Sròn na Teiste are partially Norse in origin. Possible evidence of Norse settlement on

Muck is a recently discovered large oval building at Toaluinn (or Taolun).

In the earliest account of Muck, from 1549, Sir Donald Munro, High Dean of the Isles, wrote that the island was 'very fertile and fruitful' with good fishing and 'one good Highland haven in it'. Around 1634 Donald Garve Maclean of Coll took possession of Muck from the Maclans of Ardnamurchan, whereafter he gave the island to his eldest son, Lachlan. Five MacLean lairds followed him until the late 18th century when the incumbent laird ran into debt, which was paid off by Clanranald in exchange for the island.

In 1816 MacLean of Coll bought back Muck from Clanranald's trustees. At this time, kelp farming was an important source of income for the island, but the price of kelp declined and MacLean was soon in debt. The population of Muck had reached its peak of 320: in 1828 the MacLeans evicted 150 people who were transported on the St Lawrence from Tobermory to Cape Breton. By 1835 the remaining population had either emigrated or migrated elsewhere in Scotland.

In 1896 the island was bought by Lawrence Thomson, then owner of Eigg. The farmhouse was enlarged and the present farm cottages and barns built. Thomson died in 1913 and the island passed to his brother, John MacEwen, who let the farm to tenants. In 1916, Commander William MacEwen RN inherited the island.

After his death in 1967, Muck passed to his eldest son, Alasdair, who farmed the island before moving to the mainland. The farm was taken over by his brother, Lawrence, who farms it to this day. His younger brother, Ewen, returned to the island in the early 1970s, building and establishing the Hotel at Port Mòr.

WILDLIFE

Other than livestock and Highland ponies, there are no large land mammals on Muck. Otters live and breed in small numbers around the island. Rats are numerous, many of them living around the shores and feeding on shellfish. Short-tailed voles are common, long-tailed field mice and pygmy shrews less so. There are no reptiles on Muck and the only amphibian is the common toad. Atlantic grey seals can be seen near Fionnard and Port Mòr and along the north shore, principally at Godag, Port Chreadhain and Eilean nan Each where small numbers of pups are born every autumn. Common seals occur in smaller numbers

Porpoises were once common, particularly in Gallanach Bay, and they can still be seen in the waters around Muck. Pods of dolphins can sometimes be seen and killer whales are occasionally spotted. Minke whales are regularly seen in the waters around the island between July and September. Basking sharks are seasonal visitors, feeding in the rich coastal waters.

Muck has a large number of sea-birds, which nest predominantly on Eagamol and Eilean nan Each or on the rocks and small islands offshore. Puffins also nest on Muck, but in fewer areas than in the past. There are also Manx shearwaters, guillemots, razorbills, fulmars, gannets, cormorants, shags, terns and many varieties of gull. Passage migrants are also numerous, some of which overwinter, including turnstones and bar-tailed godwits, greylag, white-fronted and brent geese.

Insect life abounds on Muck, partly because insecticides are not used on the island. The relative lack of both shelter and calm days means that midges and clegs (horse flies) are relatively scarce – a rare and wonderful phenomenon in the Inner Hebrides. Butterflies and moths are abundant and occasional rare species such as the transparent burnet moth are to be found.

WOODLAND, FLOWERS AND PLANTS

Muck is low-lying and fertile with over a hundred acres of cultivated land. Most of the island is pasture, with expanses of bracken in some areas and heather cover in Glen Martin. There is no natural woodland on Muck, but hazel and birch remains in a small peat bog at Bagh show that it was present in the distant past. Aside from a few poplars on the cliffs west of Port Mòr, Muck was treeless until 1922, when three small plantations were established to provide shelter and fuel. Subsequent plantations have incorporated the commoner British species and, provided with shelter, these have thrived. The success of the sitka spruce is evident in several towering specimens.

From late spring through summer the island has abundant plant life. Meadowsweet, flag iris, golden silverweed, thistle, bell heather, saxifrage,

Port Mòr, Isle of Muck (Walk 12) – with An Sgùrr on Eigg in the background

Port Mòr tea rooms

tormentil and various umbellifers are among the common plants encountered in the island's various habitats. Surprisingly, a few alpine plants are found, 600m below their usual altitude: dwarf juniper, crowberry, club moss, rose root sedum, mountain catspaw and pyramidal bugle. Among the less-common plants found on Muck are thyme broomrape, the frog orchid and small white orchid.

GETTING AROUND

Visitors are not permitted to bring vehicles to Muck; there is no public transport on the island and only 3km of road anyway. Getting around on foot or by bicycle are the main options.

AMENITIES

A single stone building in Port Mòr houses The Craft Shop, Tea Room and Restaurant, open every day from June to August from 11am. The tea room and restaurant serves home-made food using locally sourced produce. Dinners are served on request and should be booked well in advance, tel: 01687 462990 or 460057. The shop stocks a small range of provisions including Isle of Muck lamb, as well as art and crafts produced on the island. The Port Mòr House Hotel restaurant is open to non-residents for evening meals, booking is advised. The Green Shed craft shop in Port Mòr also sells a range of locally produced arts and crafts.

WALK 12

Around the coast of Muck

Start	Port Mòr (NM 422 794)
Distance	14km (8¾ miles)
Total Ascent	442m (1450ft)
Time	4½–5hrs
Map	OS Explorer 397: OS Landranger 39

A walk around the entire coastline of Muck takes in changing landscapes with diverse terrain and constantly shifting views of the neighbouring islands and mainland mountains. The cliffs and rugged coastal terrain at the island's west make for a remarkable contrast with the low-lying east, and the often wild and dramatic west can feel surprisingly remote. The coastal terrain is not especially demanding, though it varies from soft, springy turf to rough, boggy ground in places with a number of stock fences to be crossed, especially in the eastern and central parts of the island. There is livestock grazing throughout the island.

Walking around the entire island in one go is perfectly manageable for fit walkers but is not to be underestimated. The route can be shortened by 2.5km and as much as an hour's walk by omitting the easternmost part of Muck and walking across the island from Port Mòr to Gallanach along the rustic road, which seldom sees traffic.

Just north of Pier House, opposite the old pier, a track climbs gently south-east away from the road, passing to the right of a house. Go through a stock gate, pass a shed and two houses before turning left off the main track past allotment gardens. Continue along the track as it bends south again and passes along the outside of a fence. Go through a gate in the fence above the shore and continue, trending north-east, along low cliff tops.

Step over a fence near the cliff edge, walk a short away along the edge of a gully then continue along low cliffs again following a narrow path. Contour along staying above an area of rough, boggy ground before following a path along the edge of some ancient lazy beds to rejoin the low cliff tops as the coastline turns northwest. Continue along the coast, soon crossing a boggy area around a small burn outflowing to the cliff by an old fence. Walk on 300 metres, to arrive at a stock fence, follow it 100 metres inland and go through a gate. Continue along a faint path on boggy ground to rejoin the cliff top, soon arriving at the small headland of **Am Maol**. ▶

From the neck of Am Maol, continue past the large pebble beach at Port nam Maol, following the path through boggy ground and old lazy beds to gain higher ground. Follow the path around to a gate in a stock fence, go through to continue along the increasingly rugged coastline. Cross a burn flowing through a man-made channel and make for a drystone wall and fence where it abuts a basalt dike near the shore. Climb over the wall, turn left and go through a stock gate into a field.

This fine vantage point looks across the Sound of Eigg to the striking ridge of An Sgùrr, with Rum to the north.

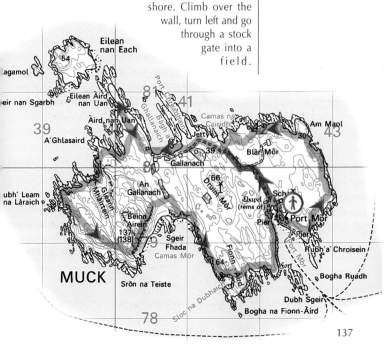

MUCK

137

Along the north coast of Muck with the long ridge of An Sgùrr on Eigg beyond (Walk 12)

Walk diagonally – south-west – across the field on a slight rise to go through another stock gate, turn right (north-west), then continue around to the point on the low cliff top at Toaluinn for the view north-west to Eilean nan Each beyond the tip of the narrow Aird nan Uan peninsula. From the point, follow the stock fence back inland to a gate. Go through, descend a little, crossing a meadow to the rear of the beach at Camas na Cairidh, making for a gate in a dry stone wall at its far side.

> The lower part of the meadow above the shore makes for a **wonderful campsite** with fine views across to Rum. The site has a permanent yurt for hire, a composting toilet and a nearby burn for fresh water.

Go through the gate, turn left and climb a short way to join the road. Turn right along the road and arrive at Gallanach Bay after 600 metres. Drop down to the beach from the road and continue around the bay, passing in front of **Gallanach** farmhouse and farm buildings. Rejoin the road and continue above a second, smaller beach to the western edge of the bay, passing by more farm buildings. Where the road ends, follow a path north above the shore along the **Aird nan Uan** peninsula towards a house perched above the shore.

Cross a fence by a step stile in front and left of the house, climb a short way, cross a wooden fence, turn right (north-west) and walk out along the peninsula following a path to the narrow isthmus connecting tide-separated **Eilean aird nan Uan**. From here there is a good view on to **Eilean Nan Each**. ▶

Retrace your steps most of the way back along the peninsula before crossing above the head of the inlet on its western side. Make for the rustic-looking grass-roofed bothy standing back from the shore.

Follow a boggy path north-west along the coast for 250 metres to arrive at a beach composed entirely of small shells. Climb a short way above the beach by a small burn and continue along the coast, soon joining a distinct path contouring along above the shore beneath low craggy cliffs. Descend a short way to cross a boggy area with several burns draining towards the shore. Climb again above the shore onto low cliffs and gain height as the coastline turns south. Continue climbing steadily on a distinct path along the increasingly dramatic cliff tops, with fine views down to the rugged coastline below and across to Ardnamurchan, Mull, Coll and Tiree to the south and south-west.

Follow the cliff top path as it descends a short way before climbing again to the high cliff top above **Sròn na Teiste**. Turn north-east along the coastline towards

It is possible to cross to the island at low tide.

Grass roofed private bothy (Walk 12)

139

the looming bulk of **Beinn Airein**. Descend a short way before climbing steeply diagonally up through a craggy cliff on a distinct path to an area of level ground before climbing steeply once again near the cliff edge to gain the summit (137m).

> Marked with a 'Vanessa' triangulation pillar, Beinn Airein makes a **fine vantage point** with 360° views across Muck and over the surrounding islands and mainland.

Descend north-east on a grassy slope avoiding rocky areas around the summit. Continue descending along the cliff top inside the stock fence. At the bottom of the descent at about 30m, go through a gate at a fence junction, which is hidden below a bluff. Continue across the neck of the jutting promontory of Torr nam Fitheach and go through gateways on either side of a dry stone walled sheepfold. Follow the course of the wall towards then parallel to the shore to arrive at a gate in the south-east corner of the field.

Go through the gate and follow the track for a short way before continuing south-south-east along a path following the coast. Go through a gate in a stock fence and continue along the cliff top to arrive above the rugged cliff-flanked inlet of **Sloc na Dubhaich**. Climb steeply a short way east to the high ground above the inlet then contour along on a path, staying above the rugged and boggy ground at the shore. Descend to cross a burn, pass through an old dry stone wall and continue around to the Bronze Age fortification known as Caisteal an Dùin Bhàin ('castle of the white fort'), which sits atop a volcanic bluff – an obvious cylindrical upthrust of rock with six metre-high vertical cliffs all round.

From Dùin Bhàin follow the path north above Port Mòr and, where it divides, climb a short way to follow the path along the higher ground, soon arriving at a track road. Follow the track road as it winds downhill passing a house and the **Port Mòr** hotel before joining the– Gallanach road a short way from the village.

COLL
Cola

Feall Bay, Coll (Walk 13) (photo: Giulia Hetherington)

The indescribably beautiful little bay at Tràigh Halum (Walk 13)

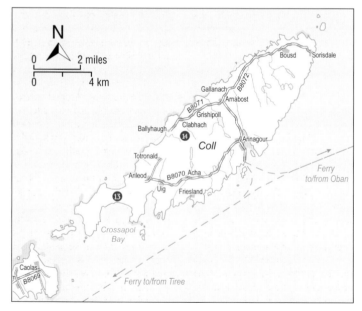

INTRODUCTION

Coll and its near neighbour, Tiree, are often referred to as the Hebridean Twins. The islands lie south-west of the Small Isles and 12km (7½ miles) west of Mull. Coll is about 30km (13 miles) long by 5km (3 miles) wide, and its highest point is Ben Hogh, rising to 104m (341ft) at the island's south-west.

The southern part of Coll is garlanded with magnificent dune-backed sandy beaches, while the north of the island is a wild and rugged landscape of rock and heather, scattered with myriad tiny lochans. Arinagour, Coll's main village, lies on the west side of Loch Eatharna, and is home to about half the island's population of 200.

The island's north is sparsely populated and beyond Sorisdale at the far north-east it is entirely uninhabited. The pier at Arinagour is the landing point for the Caledonian MacBrayne ferry, linking Coll with Tiree and the west coast port of Oban, some 75km distant. Aside from its wonderful beaches, Coll is best known for its birdlife – particularly its population of corncrakes – and for the 15th-century Breachacha Castle with its four storey rectangular tower-house, formerly a stronghold of the MacLeans.

Coll is centrally placed along the chain of Hebridean islands: Barra and South Uist are often visible to the north-west; Rum, Eigg, Muck and Skye can be seen to the north; Mull, the Treshnish Isles and the Paps of Jura to the south-east; and nearby Gunna and Tiree lie to the south-west. The vista of Hebridean islands makes a dramatic backdrop to Coll's flower-filled machairs and sparkling white shell-sand beaches. The best walking on Coll is in the island's south-west, while a series of beautiful sandy bays along the north-west coast can be linked together for pleasant strolls.

GEOLOGY

Coll is largely composed of metamorphic Lewisian gneiss – the oldest rock in Europe, at around 2500–4000 million years old. On Coll and Tiree it forms extensive outcrops of banded, granular rock, giving way in south Coll to a more varied outcrop of granite, marble and quartzite. The gneiss is essentially part of the ancient Canadian Shield, which was joined to Greenland, before north-west Europe separated from North America with the formation of the Atlantic Ocean during the Jurassic Period, approximately 150 million years ago.

At Uig, the Coll marble outcrops as thin bands of attractive green and white rock, rich in serpentine and mica minerals. At Acha there is a quartzite ridge on which the island's Iron Age inhabitants built Dùn an Achaidh fort. At Breachacha Bay the

The Clach na Ban-righ was deposited on Ben Hogh by the retreating ice sheet and is perched on three small rocks (Walk 14)

tough granulite rocks are impregnated with pegmatites – beautiful pink feldspars – and red-brown garnets. Both minerals were concentrated into these rocks under intense metamorphic heat and pressure.

The last ice to cover Coll during the Quartenary glaciation dates to the Devensian advance, some 18,000 years ago. The passage of the ice scoured and eroded the ancient gneiss bedrock to a considerable extent, leaving a much reduced landscape. As the Devensian ice melted 15,000 years ago, the sea level rose, completely inundating Coll, but the island steadily rebounded above the maximum sea level rise as the weight

of the ice was removed. This emergence has left raised beaches around Chad and Arnabost. The withdrawal of the ice sheet also left a spectacularly perched erratic boulder on Ben Hogh.

Peat deposits eventually formed, and along the western shores this soil combined with wind blown shell sands to form the island's fertile machair. In late spring and summer, the machair is covered in a multi-coloured carpet of flowers.

HISTORY

The first permanent settlement on the island dates from the Neolithic Age (4000–2000BC), when the itinerant Mesolithic hunter gatherers began settling into permanent agriculture-based communities employing new farming skills imported from mainland Europe.

Bronze Age sites include the round cairn of Cnoc a'Bhadain, which overlooks Loch Eatharna from a rocky ridge north of Arinagour; cists in the sand dunes west of Killunaig burial ground; and the standing stones at Totronald, known as Na Sgeulachan – 'The Tellers of Tales'.

There are four Iron Age (c600BC–AD400) forts on Coll, but few remains survive. The best-preserved is Dùn an Achaidh, which sits on the crest of a quartzite ridge so the gneiss boulders used to build the dun wall are easily distinguished. The wall enclosing the summit is over 2.5m thick and 1m high in places, nearby debris suggests it may have once stood 4–5m high.

The Romans recorded the earliest account of the Hebrides, following Agricola's expedition north in AD81, but it is difficult to identify Coll among the islands they describe. Around the fifth century AD, Coll was colonised by Gaels – the Scotti of Dál Riata from the north of Ireland. At the end of the eighth century the Vikings appeared in the seas around the Inner Hebrides, first as raiders then as settlers.

Coll was part of the Norse Kingdom of Man and the Isles until the early 13th century, when Norse dominance in the Inner Hebrides was ended by the Norse–Gael king,

Grass-roofed dwelling, Sorisdale

Somerled. Somerled's descendants, Clanranald – known as the Lords of the Isles – subsequently controlled the entire west coast of Scotland, which they ruled from Finlaggan on Islay for more than 150 years. The Clanranald lands were forfeit following John MacDonald II's treasonous treaty with Edward IV of England against the Scottish crown and his defeat in battle by James IV in 1493.

With the demise of the MacDonald's Lordship, Coll came into possession of the MacLeans of Mull. In 1593 the Macleans of Duart invaded their kinsmen on Coll, intending to wrest control of the island. A bloody battle ensued, and the burn flowing into Loch Breachacha filled with the heads of decapitated Duarts. The burn has been known as Struthan nan Ceann – the 'Stream of the Heads' – ever since.

By 1841, Coll's population had risen to 1440, but the laird, MacLean, was unable or unwilling to manage the land to support such numbers. The potato famine exacerbated the situation and MacLean evicted nearly half of Coll's inhabitants, who were transported to Australia and Canada. Further emigrations left Coll almost uninhabited, with too few younger people to work the land and keep a viable community. In 1858, the MacLeans of Coll sold the island to the Stewarts. Coll is now owned by a trust, the RSPB and individual farmers and crofters.

WILDLIFE

Otters patrol territories around the coastline of Coll and can be seen hunting offshore. Brown hares occur in large numbers, but there are no rabbits. Hedgehogs were recently introduced, but have not proliferated. Brown rats are present, as are field mice and pygmy shrews. Bats have been recorded. Toads are scarce on Coll, but there is a thriving frog population. Atlantic grey and common seals are seen around the coast, basking on rocks and skerries – notably around Cliad Bay. In autumn, grey seals haul out to have pups along rocky stretches of coastline, particularly around Cliad and Gallanach. Dolphins, minke whales, killer whales and basking sharks can also be seen in the waters around Coll.

Coll is popular with birdwatchers partly for the diversity it offers but also for the ferry trip through the Sound of Mull from Oban, from which Manx shearwaters, petrels, auks, diving gannets and occasional white-tailed eagles can be seen. The RSPB owns a large area of the southwest corner of Coll and the reserve was established largely to protect the rare corncrake (*Crex crex*). Merlin, hen harrier, lapwing, curlew, golden plover, redshank, twite, various divers and wintering barnacle, greylag and white-fronted geese are among the species found on Coll. Nesting seabirds include the fulmar, shag, great black-backed gull and little tern.

WOODLAND, PLANTS AND FLOWERS

Apart from a small wooded area near Arinagour, Coll is virtually treeless, largely because of the island's geology and exposed position. In late spring and summer a multicoloured explosion of flowers carpet the island's large expanses of coastal machair. Species include buttercups, bird's foot trefoil, saxifrages and carline thistle, scarlet pimpernel, eyebright, clover, thyme, wild pansy, violets, harebell, daisy, silverweed and hawkbit, mountain everlasting and gentians. In the summer months much of the island is also carpeted with orchids, including Irish ladies tresses, *Spiranthes romanzoffiana*.

The peaty soil of the island's hinterlands sustains a variety of bog plants including heather, bracken and bog myrtle, along with bog asphodel, sundews, mosses and bog cotton. Pipewort (*Eriocaulon aquaticum*) can be found in some of the more remote lochans and the only recorded examples of spotted rock-rose (*Tuberaria guttata*) in Scotland were discovered on Coll.

GETTING AROUND

There is no public transport on Coll, although there is a taxi service – Coll

Thrift or sea pinks, a common sight along Coll's coastline

The pier at Arinagour

Taxis, tel: 01879 230402. The best way to get around is by bicycle or on foot if you're not taking your own car. Bike hire is available from An Arcarsaid, the island gift shop and Post Office, tel: 01879 230395. There is a petrol station in Arinagour.

AMENITIES

Arinagour is the principal village, where the ferry arrives. Island Stores sells a variety of produce and takes advance orders from visitors, tel: 01879 230484, www.islandstores. co.uk. An Arcarsaid is a craft/gift shop, Post Office and bike hire, tel: 01879 230395, www.anacarsaid.co.uk). The Island Café offers a good variety of home-made food, tel: 01879 230262.

The Post Office has a cashpoint, which is only available during opening hours. The hotel, café and petrol station take most credit/debit cards. The store only takes cash or cheques (with guarantee card) – no credit/debit cards. There are public toilets at the pier in Arinagour. Mobile phone coverage is currently poor. The island has a resident doctor and nurse. The Medical Centre is just outside Arinagour on the road to the west end of Coll. A medical emergency requires a helicopter transfer to the mainland – weather permitting. The island has a volunteer fire service and coast-guard service. Dial 999 for emergencies. If you need the police you may have to wait for the next ferry or, in a real emergency, for the helicopter to arrive.

WALK 13
Coll's western tip

Start	Coll Nature Reserve car park (NM 151 538)
Distance	14.5km (9 miles): 9km (5½ miles) or 12km (7½ miles) with shortcuts
Total Ascent	205m (670ft)
Time	4–5hrs, shorter alternatives possible
Map	OS Explorer 372: OS Landranger 46

This circular route around the Coll Nature Reserve traverses the entire low-lying coastline of Coll's western tip, visiting several sublime dune-backed beaches, the vantage point of Ben Feall and the exposed, windy westernmost extremity of Calgary Point, with fine views across Caolas Bàn to Gunna and Tiree. The going is mostly easy along shell sand beaches, springy machair and marram grass-matted sand dunes, although the route does also cross some rocky and boggy ground. This is a route to savour: there are abundant birds and wild flowers to admire, beautiful white sand bays with sparkling amethyst waters and magnificent views in every direction. There are two shortcuts described.

From the car park, follow the grassy track north, passing an enormous boulder after 600 metres. The track soon bends north-west then forks at the foot of **Ben Feall** (66m) after 1km. Take the right hand path to climb the hill. ▶ Retrace your steps down the hill then turn right along the track to arrive at the eastern end of Feall Bay. Make your way along the 1.5km sweep of **Feall Bay** – look out for otters patrolling the water.

At the western end of the bay, climb a little above the beach, go through a gate and follow a vague path a short way north-west. A signpost indicates 'Calgary Point 4½ km' to the south-west. Continue, following the path – there are occasional waymark posts – south-west along or parallel to the coast for 2km before arriving at a signpost with one arrow pointing north-west, indicating 'Calgary Point

The summit gives wonderful views across the western end of Coll with the magnificent white sand crescent of Tràigh Feall fringing Feall Bay below to the south-west.

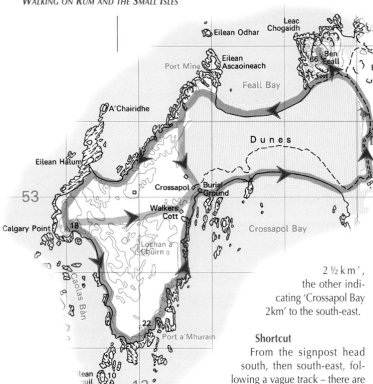

Leac Chogaidh

Eilean Odhar

Eilean Ascaoineach

Port Mìne

Ben Feall
66

Feall Bay

A'Chairidhe

Dunes

Eilean Halum

Crossapol

Burial Ground

Walkers Cott

53

Crossapol Bay

Calgary Point

18

Lochan a Chuirn

Caolas Bàn

22

Port a'Mhurain

ilean uil
10

12

2 ½ k m ', the other indicating 'Crossapol Bay 2km' to the south-east.

Shortcut

From the signpost head south, then south-east, following a vague track – there are occasional waymarkers and signposts (follow 'Crossapol Bay'). The track becomes more distinct and passes by Crossapol House and its farm buildings: follow a track down to the shore at Tràigh Garbh. Resume the main route from here.

Continue initially north-west for Calgary Point, go through a stock gate after 150 metres and continue, shortly crossing a stock fence via a step stile. Turn to follow the coast south-west, soon arriving above the lovely beach of Tràigh Halum, a beautiful white sand arc that terminates in the rocky outcrop of **Eilean Halum**. A marker post above the

bay points south-west, but descend to walk around the bay before climbing above the shore again and following the coastline around to the south-west, arriving at the triangulation pillar on **Calgary Point** after a further 1km.

Looking down on Feall Bay from Ben Feall

Calgary Point can be a windy spot, but the **view south-west** across Caolas Bàn to Gunna with Tiree across Gunna Sound beyond is sublime and occasionally dramatic when the tide comes roaring through the narrow strait. To the south the coastline extends away in a series of dune-backed, white sand beaches fringed by sparkling jade-green waters.

Shortcut
From Calgary Point, head east-north-east, initially through dunes then traversing rougher, occasionally boggy ground, using gates to pass through stock fences en route. Make for a point just to the north of Walker's Cottage – the first of two houses along the coast here – and go through a gate to join the track leading north-east to Crossapol House. From here follow the main route.

From Calgary Point continue initially south-east to Tràigh nan Sìolag, either dropping down to the beach or continuing along the edge of the dunes. Continue

Walking towards Tràigh nan Sìolag

for 1.5km to arrive at the southernmost point of the peninsula.

Come above the shore and continue north-east along the coast on undemanding terrain. Pass around **Port a' Mhùrain** and cut across the neck of Rubha nan Faochag; the terrain becomes rockier as you continue north-east, passing the inlets of Port Bàn and Port an Duine and crossing a couple of stock fences en route. Continue along the coast, keeping seaward of a stock fence running parallel to the shore as you approach Walker's Cottage. Pass around the rocky inlet in front of the cottage and continue along the coast to the cemetery in front of **Crossapol** House.

Join the track in front of the house and follow it around and down to the western extremity of Tràigh Garbh. Continue along the beach or dune edge for 700 metres before passing the rocky outcrop of Sgeir Dubh to arrive on the expansive white sand arc of Tràigh Crossapol. The beach is around 1.5km long and can seem much longer – in a good way. Near the south-eastern extremity of the bay take the sandy track up through the low dunes and follow it for 1km back to the Nature Reserve car park.

WALK 14

Ben Hogh and the Breachacha castles

Start	B8071 by Clabhach cottages (GR 181 587)
Distance	17km (10½ miles), 13.5km (8½ miles) with shortcut
Total Ascent	280m (920ft)
Time	5–6hrs, 4–4½hrs with shortcut
Map	OS Explorer 372: OS Landranger 046

This route crosses the island from north coast to south coast, by way of Ben Hogh (104m) – Coll's highest point – an inland sea of sand dunes, the dune-backed inlet of Port an t-Saoir and the north coast vantage point of Ben Feall (66m) before crossing the island's narrow neck to arrive at the eccentric Breachacha castles perched at the head of Loch Breachacha. The return retraces some of the outward route and also visits the superlative Hebridean beach of Tràigh Hogh, fringing Hogh Bay near the walk's end. A shortcut cuts 3.5km (2 miles) off the route.

Climbing Ben Hogh, with the Clac na Ban-righ boulder and Clabhach below

From Clabhach cottages, go through a stock gate by the bend in the road and initially follow an old track south-east then south. Pass to the right of an enormous boulder with a ruined croft house to your right. Follow a vague path over boggy ground making for a step stile set in a dry stone wall. Go over and climb a short way to gain the north ridge of **Ben Hogh**. Climb south to the hill's northern top then make for the curious and impressive boulder perched daintily on three small rocks.

> The **Clach na Ban-righ** ('The Queen's Rock') was probably deposited in its unlikely situation by the retreating ice sheet at the end of the last glacial period, but tradition has it that the huge boulder came to rest high on Ben Hogh during a game played by a giant and his mistress when they were using the rocks as balls.

Continue to the summit of Ben Hogh, which enjoys 360° views across the island and beyond – look north-east for fine views of Rum and Eigg. Walk south-west a short way to cross a stile over a stock fence. Descend a short way across a rock outcrop then follow a dry stone wall

Hogh Bay

down the south-western flank of the hill. At around 60m turn north-west to pass beneath a steep rock outcrop. Descend towards the corner of a field at the southern end of the little loch by **Ballyhaugh**, where a gate is hidden behind a rocky knoll. Go through the gate, then another across the field, cross a small burn on a rickety footbridge and turn left onto the sandy track heading south-west into the dunes. The collection of white buildings is the Hebridean Centre.

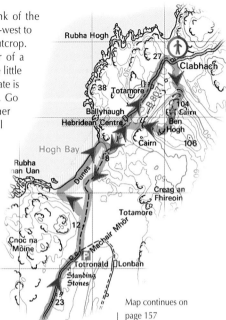

Continue along the track and soon catch a glimpse of **Hogh Bay** – keep straight ahead on the track for now and save Tràigh Hogh for the return. The track meanders through the dunes for 2km

Map continues on page 157

before reaching a stock gate; go through, pass a small parking area and continue along the track road. ◄

The road soon passes the RSPB visitor centre at **Totronald**. This is well worth a visit, not least for the impressive collection of whale bones piled outside. Continue along the track road as it climbs a little and passes by Na Sgeulachan – 'The Tellers of Tales' – an impressive pair of standing stones a short way off the road to the left. After a further 1.5km, the track road joins the B8070 at **Arileod**. Continue straight ahead past a left hand turn then look out for a track on the right heading west from the road – a small sign indicates 'Footpath to Port an t-Saoir'.

Shortcut

To miss out Port an t-Saoir and Ben Feall, continue straight ahead along the B8070; the road soon bends sharply right (west) then crosses a cattle grid next to a house at The Roundhouse. Turn left on an old tarmacked

This is a good area for hearing – if not actually seeing – corncrakes with their creaking call.

The 'old' Breachacha castle

track and continue south for 750 metres before taking a track on your left leading to the 'new' **Breachacha Castle**.

Follow the track west for just over 1km to arrive at the dune-backed sandy inlet of Port an t-Saoir, which is flanked on its west side by the bulk of Ben Feall. After exploring the beach, continue south along the track for 400 metres to a path junction. Turn right then right again to make the short climb to the summit of **Ben Feall** (66m). ▶

Retrace your steps down the hill then continue south-east on a grassy track, passing an enormous boulder before arriving at the Coll Nature Reserve car park after 1km. Take the second track on your left heading east through a stock gate. Continue east for 750 metres, passing through two more gates before arriving by the farm at Carpach. Turn left, continue north for 200 metres, then turn right on a track leading to the 'new' **Breachacha Castle**.

This vantage point gives wonderful views across the western end of Coll with the magnificent white sand crescent of Tràigh Feall fringing Feall Bay below to the south-west.

The 'new' **castle**, built in 1750 by Hector MacLean, was visited by Boswell and Johnson on their Hebridean tour in October 1773. They were entertained by the MacLeans' last hereditary piper, but having been confined to quarters by gales, they seem not to have enjoyed their visit. The 'old' Breachacha Castle on the shore of Loch Breachacha is a good, little-altered example of a

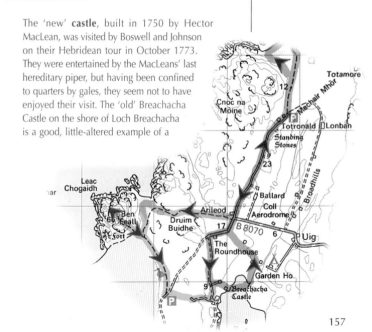

Medieval fortress. It was probably the seat of the MacLeans and part of the defences of the Lordship of the Isles. Recent excavations suggest a 15th-century construction.

Walk towards the abandoned-looking Georgian castle then take a track to your right leading to a stock gate. Go through and head towards the old castle; cross a stock fence by a stile and then go through a stock gate to exit onto the beach. Skirt around the beach and cross the outflow of the Struthan nan Ceann – the 'Stream of the Heads' – wherever is easiest.

After exploring the bay, head north towards a weather-boarded house sitting 250 metres back from the beach, crossing the river wherever is easiest. From the front of the house, follow a grassy track winding north-west for 500 metres to a stock gate. Go through to rejoin the B8070 at a sharp bend in the road. Continue straight ahead (north-east) and retrace the outward route for 2km, passing **Totronald**. Go through the stock gate by the parking area and continue north along the track through the dunes. After 500 metres turn left at a cross in the track and continue north-west through the dunes for a further 500 metres before arriving at the south-western end of **Hogh Bay**. Walk along the 1km-long bay. At its north-east end, turn right, cross a burn to rejoin the track. Continue north-east through a gate and onwards to the Hebridean Centre, passing through two gates to rejoin the B8071. Follow the road for 1km back to Clabhach.

TIREE
Tir Iodh

Weathered rock near Port Snoig (Walk 16)

INTRODUCTION

Tiree lies south-west of Coll, west of Mull and is the most westerly of the Inner Hebrides – 35km (22 miles) west of Ardnamurchan, the nearest point on the Scottish mainland. It is relatively small – just over 16km (10 miles) at its longest, 8km (5 miles) at its widest, and a kilometre at its narrowest – and very flat. Tiree's highest point is Carnan Mòr on Ben Hynish (141m), rising above the island's south-western end. Much of the 74km (46 miles) of coastline is fringed with white shell sand beaches. The tamer of the Hebridean Twins, Tiree offers a gentler proposition for

walkers than her more rugged sibling; much of the coastline – comprising sand dunes, machair and white sandy bays – can be walked over the course of several day walks.

Tiree has a population of around 800. The main village and harbour is at Scarinish, where ferries sail to and from Arinagour on Coll and Oban on the mainland, as well as once weekly to Castlebay on Barra. Tiree Airport is at nearby Crossapol. The island is highly fertile and the machair makes for good farming and crofting, which alongside tourism are the main

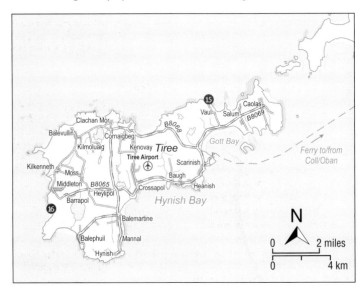

Looking down on Port Snoig from Tiree's southern cliffs (Walk 16)

sources of employment. The island's name derives from the Gaelic *Tir Iodh*, meaning 'the land of corn'.

Tiree has a mild climate and records among the highest total hours of sunshine anywhere in the British Isles during late spring and early summer. The island benefits from the moderating influence of the Gulf Stream, ensuring that frosts are rare and mid-summer evenings are warm and balmy. Owing to its exposed situation, Tiree is an exceptionally windy island: the prevailing south-westerlies bring a succession of weather systems from the Atlantic. There are gales on average 34 days a year, the fiercest in December and January. A happy consequence of Tiree's windy disposition is that midges are almost non-existent. Tiree is also a magnet for windsurfers.

The island is known for its vernacular architecture, including 'blackhouses' and 'white houses', many

retaining their traditional thatched roofs, as well as its unique 'pudding' or 'spotted houses' where only the mortar is painted white. Tiree has a considerable percentage of Gaelic speakers (48.6 per cent from the 2001 Census, which is high for the Inner Hebrides).

GEOLOGY

Tiree is essentially composed of the metamorphic Lewisian gneiss also found on the Outer Hebrides, Coll, Iona, Islay and a coastal strip of mainland Scotland extending from Cape Wrath to the Kyle of Lochalsh. At 2500–4000 million years old, these are the oldest rocks in the British Isles and among the oldest on the planet. Lewisian gneisses were formed many kilometres beneath the earth's crust under great temperature and pressure. Tiree's incredibly hard metamorphic basement rocks have been subjected to the stresses of colliding tectonic plates, continental break-up and the uplift of mountain ranges. The resultant fracturing is visible in displaced bands within the rocks.

Basalt intrusions in the gneiss were formed in the Lower Tertiary period, around 56 million years ago, when volcanic magma filled cracks in the Earth's crust radiating out from centres of eruption in Mull and Ardnamurchan. On Tiree, these basalt veins are often worn down below the level of the harder gneiss, whereas the surrounding Lewisian rocks remain.

The last ice to cover Tiree dates to the Devensian advance, some 18,000 years ago. The passage of the ice scoured and eroded the land, smoothing rock exposures. The advancing glacier carried 'erratics' – rocks displaced to places where they don't occur in the bedrock. The Ringing Stone, perched on the island's north coast, is a light grey granodiorite boulder carried from Rum.

As the Devensian ice melted around 15,000 years ago, the sea level rose, completely inundating Tiree, but the island steadily rebounded above the maximum sea level rise as the weight of the ice was removed. There are raised beaches at several locations around Tiree, including Kilmoluaig and between Ruaig and Milton.

Glacial meltwaters also swept vast quantities of sand and gravel into the sea, spreading the debris over much of what is now the continental shelf. As the sea level rose, a mixture of glacial sediment and tiny fragments of crushed mollusc shells was swept ashore by wind and wave action, forming Tiree's characteristic white sand beaches and coastal sand dunes.

Gneiss is non-porous so the low-lying land in the middle of the island is often wet. Over thousands of years, decomposing vegetation formed thick layers of peat on the bedrock. The peaty soil combined with wind-blown shell sand to form the basis of

The Ringing Stone is a glacial erratic originating on Rum and bearing 53 cup marks (Walk 15)

the fertile, well-drained, flower-rich grassland known as machair. The Reef is one of the largest expanses of wet machair in the world and in summer it is covered in a multi-coloured riot of flowers.

HISTORY

On Tiree's north coast, between Balephetrish and Vaul, a large glacial erratic boulder known as the Ringing Stone – it emits a metallic ringing sound when struck – has a number of characteristic 'cup marks' dating from the Neolithic Age (4000–2000BC). Other Neolithic traces include stone circles and chambered tombs.

Bronze Age culture reached Tiree around 4000 years ago. The islanders erected standing stones, including two stone circles at Hough. There are Bronze Age graves at sites including Cnoc an Fhoimheir, in Kirkapol.

There are remains of over 20 Iron Age (c600BC–AD400) forts on Tiree, mostly perched on inaccessible vantage points. The best examples are Dùn na Cleite at Happy Valley near Hynish and Dùn Shiadair by West Hynish. There are also two Iron Age brochs on Tiree: Dùn Mòr Bhalla is the only prehistoric structure on Tiree to have been properly excavated, while Dùn Mòr a' Chaolais stands on the hill above Milton harbour.

From early in the third century an Irish tribe – Scotti of Dál Riata – began the colonisation of Argyll and the Inner Hebrides. Following in their wake, Columba and his Celtic Christian missionaries founded a monastery on Iona in AD563. Around AD565, a monastic settlement known as Maigh Luinge was established on Tiree by Baithéne, the Abbot of Iona, possibly either at the site of the graveyard at Soroby or around the old chapels at Kirkapol.

In AD794, Iona suffered the first of many Viking raids, which gradually forced the monastery into decline. The Norsemen attacked Tiree for the first time soon after, returning to Norway with slaves, treasure and tales of Tiree's green farmland. Having first come as raiders, the Norsemen began to over-winter then settle in the Hebrides. Norse settlers likely took over the best farms on the island they called Tyrvist. Over half the township names are Norse, including Scarinish, Barrapol and Cornaig.

The Norsemen ruled the Hebrides until they were usurped by the Norse–Gael king, Somerled, in 1156. Somerled's descendants, Clanranald – known as the Lords of the Isles – gained control of the entire west coast of Scotland, which they ruled for 150 years. After the Lordship came to an end ownership of Tiree passed to the MacLeans in 1517 and then to the Campbells in 1674.

During the 1715 Jacobite uprising, John Campbell, 2nd Duke of Argyll commanded the government forces that defeated the Earl of Mar's army at Sherriffmuir. The following year, 358 Tiree men who had fought for the Jacobite cause were disarmed by the duke's representative in Scarinish. Tiree men were involved in the 1745 Jacobite Rebellion and following Bonnie Prince Charlie's defeat at Culloden, 30 government soldiers were sent to Tiree to punish the rebels.

By the 1700s the population of Tiree numbered 1500. The islanders were self-sufficient, with home-grown oats, barley, potatoes, milk and fish, while exporting 300 gallons of whisky and 260 cattle a year. The population peaked at almost 4500 during the 1830s due to agricultural innovation, especially the introduction of the potato crop and the development of kelp farming. However, the price of kelp declined and potato harvests failed, provoking a spate of emigration from 1848–1852. In 1849 alone, 600 people left Tiree for Canada. Some of the migrants were offered grants to leave, but the Duke of Argyll also forcibly evicted 40 families. By 1890 the population had declined to 2500 and stood at 1825 in 1912. The decline continued through the 20th century and by 1970 the population stablised at about 800.

During the Second World War, a large RAF airfield was built at The Reef – the low-lying area near the centre of Tiree – and the island experienced a large influx of forces personnel from many allied countries. After the war, the airfield became the civil airport.

WILDLIFE
Otters have territories around Tiree's coastline and are most often seen hunting just offshore. Brown hares occur in large numbers, but Tiree is also the largest rabbit-free island in Britain. Hedgehogs were recently introduced, but have not proliferated. There are brown rats, as well as field mice and pygmy shrews, on the island. Bats of indeterminate species have also been spotted. Toads are scarce, but the frog population has increased dramatically in recent years.

Grey seals are numerous around the coast and can be seen basking on the many offshore islets and skerries, off West Hynish in particular. Common seals haunt the calmer waters in the bays at Vaul and Salum, as well as Gunna Sound. Basking sharks are increasingly common in the shallow seas around Tiree. Harbour porpoises are the commonest cetacean and can be seen year-round. Occasional bottle-nosed dolphins are seen, while common dolphins can appear in large numbers during May and June particularly. Minke whales, killer whales and larger dolphins – such as Risso's, white-beaked and white-sided – are sometimes seen in deeper waters south-west of Coll or around the entrance to the Sound of Mull.

A public hide at Loch Bhasapol provides good birdwatching. During April and May the loch is home to many breeding ducks including mallard, teal and shoveler, large numbers of greylag geese, a pair of mute swans and dozens of pairs of snipe, redshank and lapwing. The reed beds are home to sedge warblers, reed buntings, black-headed gulls and Arctic terns. Spring migrants include black-tailed godwits, sand martins and swifts. In winter, Arctic-nesting wildfowl, including tufted ducks, widgeon, goldeneye and whooper swans appear in large numbers: wintering coots, small numbers of little grebes and moorhens can also be seen.

In summer, the grasslands and flower-rich machair attract many butterflies, including green-veined white, small tortoiseshell, meadow brown and common blue. Some years large numbers of painted ladies and red admirals arrive from further south. Large whites and occasional peacock butterflies are sometimes seen during June and July. Tiree's wetlands provide habitat for a small range of dragonflies and damselflies. Seven species of bumblebee thrive on Tiree – owing to the low-intensity crofting agriculture – and play a vital role in pollinating the myriad flowers on the island's machair and grasslands. The island has high densities of bees that are now scarce on the mainland.

PLANTS AND FLOWERS
Tiree is treeless largely because of its low-lying, windswept nature The island's large tracts of machair erupt into bloom in May, building to a floral crescendo in July. Species include buttercups, bird's foot trefoil, saxifrages and carline thistle, scarlet pimpernel, eyebright, clover, thyme, wild pansy, violets, harebell, daisy, silverweed and hawkbit, mountain everlasting, gentians and orchids.

GETTING AROUND
A Postbus service operates around the island, including to and from the airport. The timetable is available at Scarinish Post Office.

Hough Bay (Walk 16)

Tiree also has a Ring n' Ride service available to all, provided by Argyll and Bute Council. This service is available on demand anywhere on the island between 7am and 6pm, Monday to Saturday, tel: 01879 220419 (bookable from one week to one hour in advance).

Bike hire is available from Tiree Cycle Centre, tel: 01879 220 421, and from Mrs Judith Boyd at Millhouse, Cornaigmore, tel: 01879 220435. Car and bike hire is available from MacLennan Motors, by the ferry terminal, tel: 01879 220555. Car hire is available from Tiree Motor Company, tel: 01879 220469. A taxi service, minibus and coach hire is available from John Kennedy Taxis in Crossapol, tel: 01879 220419 (advance booking required).

AMENITIES

You can get internet access at the Rural Centre in Crossapol, open Monday to Saturday, 10am–4pm. There are public toilets at Scarinish and the Rural Centre at Crossapol. Mobile phone network coverage is limited: buying a Vodafone SIM card is a popular fix for visitors. Public telephones are available at Balephuil, Balevullin, Baugh, Caolas, Cornaigmore, Crossapol, Heylipol, Kenovay, Mannal, Middleton, Pierhead, Scarinish and

Kite surfers take advantage of windy conditions at Gott Bay

Vaul Road End – but most don't accept coins or cards.

There's a doctor at Baugh Surgery, open Monday to Friday, 8:30am–11am, no appointment necessary; Saturday 9am–11am, no appointment necessary; Monday, Wednesday, Friday 3pm–5pm, appointments only, tel: 01879 220323. For the District Nurse tel: 01879 220500. Police are at the Police Station, Scarinish, tel: 01879 220366. For Coastguard emergencies, tel: 999; for non-emergencies tel: 01475 7229988.

The Royal Bank of Scotland in Scarinish is open Monday, Tuesday, Thursday, Friday 9.15am–4.45pm, Wednesday 10.00am–4.45pm, and is closed 12.30pm–1.30pm. There are Post Offices in Scarinish, Balinoe and Cornaig, a Co-op supermarket in Scarinish, open Monday to Saturday 8am–8pm, Sunday 11am–6pm. Skinners of Tiree in Crossapol sells almost everything, although no food except fruit and vegetables, open Monday to Saturday, 11am–6pm, Sunday, 2pm–4pm; tel: 01879 220666. There are restaurants at the island's hotels, Cèabhar guest house (see Appendix B) and Elephant's End at Kirkapol, which specialises in local produce, tel: 01879 220 694, www.elephantsend.com.

WALK 15

Tiree's east coast

Start	Balephetrish Farm, Balephetrish Bay (NM 013 474)
Distance	25km (15½ miles), 13km (8 miles) with shortcut; finishing at Scarinish saves 2.5km
Total Ascent	177m (580ft)
Time	6–7hrs, 3–4hrs with shortcut
Map	OS Explorer 372: OS Landranger 046

This route takes the best part of a day and traverses the entire coastline of East Tiree, taking in a wonderful coastal fringe of sweeping white sand bays, flower-strewn machair and ancient monuments. The shorter version involves many of the highlights of the longer route and can be tackled in half a day.

It is a route well-suited to the sunny and windy conditions prevailing on Tiree from late spring to late summer, but also makes for a bracing walk in less clement conditions. However, the low-lying terrain affords no protection whatsoever from the full force of the elements – hence this is not a walk for stormy weather.

Along the coast on Gunna Sound (Walk 15)

The Ringing Stone

Follow the track road signposted for Balephetrish that turns right off the B8068. Continue towards the farm: a signpost points west, indicating 'Path to Ringing Stone'. Follow the track past houses adorned with buoys and fishing floats, turn right and go through a stock gate with a white arrow way-marker. ▶

Continue north then north-east through a second gate then another above the north-eastern end of the bay. Continue along the coast through more gates as Rum and Eigg come into view. Pass to the south of Loch Aulaig – in truth a small lochan – through two more gates; the second, above a small beach, has a way-marker indicating 'Ringing Stone 300m'. The **Ringing Stone** perches near the shore.

The fields here are grazed by livestock and the corncrake's creaking call can be heard in spring and summer.

> **The Ringing Stone** (Gaelic: *Clach a' Choire*) is so called as it emits a range of resonant metallic tones when struck with stones. It's an erratic boulder carried from the isle of Rum – 56km (35 miles) to the north – by the ice during the last glacial period. The

Map continues on
page 172

light grey granodiorite boulder is much younger
than Tiree's ancient Lewisian gneiss.

The stone is decorated with dozens of cup
marks – 53 to be exact – which date back 4000
years and are believed to have religious signifi-
cance, but their precise purpose and meaning is
unknown. Tradition has it that the stone was thrown
by a giant from Mull – should it ever be removed
from Tiree the island will sink below the waves and
be lost forever.

Continue following the meandering path along the
coastal machair, which makes for easy going on the

springy turf – watch out for occasional boggy patches. Walk around the beach at Am Beannan Ruadh and cross a fence-topped dry stone wall where it abuts a rocky outcrop. Continue south-east past the rocky outcrop and then trend east across open ground to pick up a track heading north-east below a fence-topped wall. As the track descends gently, an area of raised ground to the left is topped by the remains of **Dùn Mór** broch, an Iron Age fortification.

The **broch's** 4m-thick walls would have been perhaps 8m high and still stand to a height of 2m. The stonework in the well-preserved ground floor gallery between the outer and inner walls is thought to date from the first century BC and the discovery of Norse artefacts at the site point to occupation 1000 years after it was built.

Continue along the track and cross a fence using a stile next to a gate. The track bears right and climbs a little, but it is worth carrying straight on 200 metres to the site of Dùn Beag, which has fantastic views onto Vaul and Salum bays. Rejoin the path and climb a little past a couple of houses and just before the track swings right through a gateway, turn left on a grassy track which descends toward the shore.

Shortcut

To follow the shorter variant, continue through the gateway and follow the track road south-east for 1.5km to join the B8069 Gott–Caolas road. At the junction continue straight over to the beach at Gott Bay, turn right and continue for 2km along **Tràigh Mhòr**. At the south-western end of the bay, go through a wooden gate near a large shed to reach the B8068. Scarinish is 1km south-east along the road. To return to Balephetrish, continue north-west along the road for 3.5km.

Walk on past a house then through a stone gateway and follow the track down to the beach to continue along the sandy shore at beautiful **Vaul Bay**. At the eastern end of the bay, climb a little up and over a rocky outcrop to **Salum Bay**. Continue around the bay, climbing a little to cross a stock fence on the way. At the end of the bay, pass to the left of the farmhouse just above the shore. Go through a wooden fence next to a stock gate and continue along the track for the next 1.5km, passing through stock gates en route. Where the track reaches the farmhouse at **Miodar**, go through an old gate in a fence to your left rather than following the track around to the right of the house. Continue around the peninsula at **Urvaig** to enjoy the views over Gunna Sound to the eponymous small island with the dunes of south-eastern Coll beyond.

Looking across Gunna Sound to Gunna, with Coll beyond

At **Carraig Mhòr** several man-made stone ridges cross the pebble beach above the shore. These ridges are found around Tiree and were once used for drying kelp – the long-stemmed brown sea-weeds that surround Tiree in enormous quantities.

Kelp farming was once Tiree's most important industry after crofting and farming. In the 18th century it was discovered that soda and potash – essential to the soap and glass industries – could be recovered from some seaweeds. In summer, the kelp was dried on the stone ridges then burnt in pits and pounded into lumps with kelp irons. The pit was then covered in turf and the cooled ash cakes were collected the following day.

Walk on along the coast, pass through a gate and descend to the beach by a house at Dunbeg. Continue along the shore as the tide allows and soon cross a stock fence on a step stile before passing through gates in front of a house, either side of a small promontory at **Port Ruadh**. Pass around the edge of a small pebble beach, go through a stock gate then cross a fence by a step stile. Continue along a fine beach towards **Rubha Dubh**, cross a fence and continue along the machair as the coastline turns south, passing a house at **Rosgill**.

Walk on and soon cross a fence by a stock gate, continue past the house at Cnoc na Bothaig – the ground can be boggy here – and continue south following a line of telegraph poles through rocky and heathery terrain down to **Port Bàn**. Pass in front of a cottage with ruined outbuildings and continue through rocky and heathery terrain a short way back from the rocky coastline.

The coast soon turns west: pass by Loch an Air and 200 metres further on pass a small raised beach above an inlet to go through a wooden gate. Follow a vague path towards a house and turn right onto a track. Continue along the track, which soon becomes a tarmac road, and after 500 metres turn left off the road on to a track road leading around to a pier laden with fishing boat paraphernalia. Go through a gate where the track road ends above the pier and immediately turn right and back on yourself to follow an old track that can be a boggy morass after wet weather.

Continue along the track for 1km until it turns sharply north-west, turn left and continue next to a fence-topped dry stone wall for 200 metres. Where the wall turns sharply south-east, cross a small burn and follow the fence around the head of an inlet at **Acarsaid an Dùin** – along the shore as the tide allows. At a fence junction, cross the fence at the obvious point and continue around to Port Sgibinis. Go through a stock gate and descend to the beach at Tràigh Crìonaig.

Continue south-east along the beach for 400 metres, pass around **Rubh a' Phuirt Bhig** onto the 4km-long sandy expanse of **Tràigh Mhòr**, which curves in a huge elipse around **Gott Bay**. Walk along this endless sandy fringe to reach the south-western extremity of the beach. ◄

There are often windsurfers and kite-surfers whizzing around in the bay.

Go through a wooden gate near a large shed to reach the B8068. **Scarinish** is 1km south-east along the road. To return to Balephetrish, continue north-west along the road for 3.5km.

WALK 16

Tiree's west coast and three highest points

Start	Hynish (NL 985 393)
Distance	29km (18 miles), shorter variant: 19.5km (12 miles)
Total Ascent	686m (2250ft)
Time	7–8hrs, 5–6hrs with shortcut
Map	OS Explorer 372: OS Landranger 46

This route traverses much of Tiree's west coast, visiting an array of astonishingly beautiful, white sand, dune-backed beaches, as well as the island's three highest points – the twin tops of Carnan Mòr (141m) on Ben Hynish, Beinn Ceann a' Mhara (119m) and Beinn Hough (103m). The route also passes a number of sites of historical interest – ancient and more recent – and there are fine bird-watching opportunities along the way. From late spring to late summer, the coastal machair is awash with wild flowers.

Much of the walk is along sandy bays, marram grass-thatched sand dunes and springy-turfed coastal machair. The three climbs are relatively modest and undemanding, though the hill terrain is rocky, and boggy in places with dense heather cover. The full route makes for a lengthy walk, though there are options for shortening the route. A good alternative is to end the walk on returning to Sandaig – if you can arrange transport or have booked the Tiree 'dial-a-ride' bus (day time only) on 01879 22041. Book well in advance and allow plenty of time to arrive at Sandaig.

At Hynish the B8066 comes to an end a short distance beyond the old signalling tower, now home to the Skerryvore Lighthouse Museum.

The **Skerryvore Lighthouse Museum** houses displays and artefacts relating to the construction of the 48m-high Skerryvore lighthouse, which stands upon a rock some 17km off the coast of Tiree to the south-west. Skerryvore lighthouse was built with some difficulty between 1838 and 1844 by Alan Stevenson of the famed Stevenson engineering

175

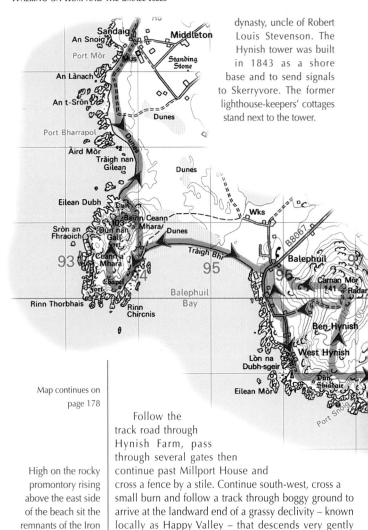

dynasty, uncle of Robert Louis Stevenson. The Hynish tower was built in 1843 as a shore base and to send signals to Skerryvore. The former lighthouse-keepers' cottages stand next to the tower.

Map continues on page 178

High on the rocky promontory rising above the east side of the beach sit the remnants of the Iron Age hillfort of Dùn nan Cleite.

Follow the track road through Hynish Farm, pass through several gates then continue past Millport House and cross a fence by a stile. Continue south-west, cross a small burn and follow a track through boggy ground to arrive at the landward end of a grassy declivity – known locally as Happy Valley – that descends very gently south-west between rugged Lewisian gneiss outcrops to the fine little beach by Clèit Mhòr. ◀

The radar station on Ben Hynish

From the beach, climb northwards a short way to around 40m, then continue contouring around the coast following a vague path; pass above **Port Snoig** and soon pass **Dùn Shiader** atop its rocky promontory.

Climb a short way to meet a dry stone wall then follow it as it climbs north-east on to **Ben Hynish**. The ground can be boggy and heathery in places, but you will soon arrive on the lower summit (126m) with the 'golf ball' radar station atop **Carnan Mòr** – Tiree's highest point – a short way to the north. Continue following the wall, descending a little then climbing briefly on the radar station access road to the summit triangulation pillar (141m). ▸

There are good views across the island on a clear day.

177

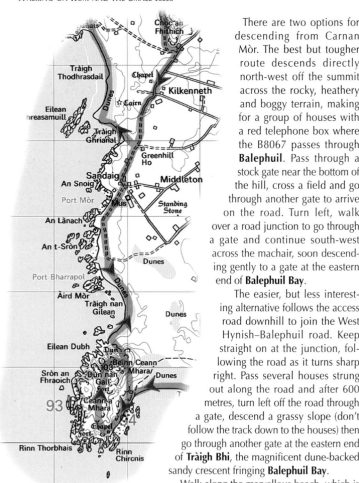

There are two options for descending from Carnan Mòr. The best but tougher route descends directly north-west off the summit across the rocky, heathery and boggy terrain, making for a group of houses with a red telephone box where the B8067 passes through **Balephuil**. Pass through a stock gate near the bottom of the hill, cross a field and go through another gate to arrive on the road. Turn left, walk over a road junction to go through a gate and continue south-west across the machair, soon descending gently to a gate at the eastern end of **Balephuil Bay**.

The easier, but less interesting alternative follows the access road downhill to join the West Hynish–Balephuil road. Keep straight on at the junction, following the road as it turns sharp right. Pass several houses strung out along the road and after 600 metres, turn left off the road through a gate, descend a grassy slope (don't follow the track down to the houses) then go through another gate at the eastern end of **Tràigh Bhi**, the magnificent dune-backed sandy crescent fringing **Balephuil Bay**.

Walk along the marvellous beach, which is framed at its western extremity by the headland of **Ceann a' Mhara**. Cross the outflow of the Abhainn a' Bhèidhe and continue either along the shore or up along the edge of the dunes to the far end of the bay. Leave the beach and follow a track onto the flat grassy area beneath

Map continues on page 180

Bein Ceann a' Mhara from Tràigh nan Gilean

the eastern flank of the headland. After 200 metres or so climb west on to the high ground towards the southern end of the headland. ▶

Continue north staying at around 50m before gaining the southern ridge of **Beinn Ceann a' Mhara**. Climb north on rocky ground to gain the summit (103m), with fine views across Balephuil Bay to Carnan Mòr. Continue a short way north, crossing a stock fence. ▶

Cross another fence and make your way over a narrow bealach onto the north ridge. Follow the ridge down as it curves north-west, joining a path at the bottom of the descent then turning right through a gate to arrive on **Tràigh nan Gilean**. Continue along the beach for 800 metres, then head up through the dunes to join a path that winds its way north above the shore. Turn left where the path intersects with a pebble-metalled track and continue north across the machair for 1km to meet the road at **Sandaig**.

Turn left to follow the road for around 600 metres then turn left off the road to descend gently along a grass track towards the shore. Cross a burn on stepping stones and continue along the shore at **Tràigh Ghrianal** as the tide allows – you may have to climb a little over dunes to reach the 1200m-long beach of **Tràigh Thodhrasdail**.

Here, at around 50m, is the site of St Patrick's Chapel – a lonely outpost of the early Christian era.

At the north end of the summit ridge, the views are fantastic along the west coast of Tiree with Tràigh nan Gilean immediately below looking very much like paradise on a sunny day.

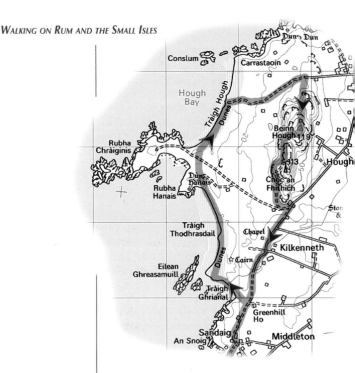

Walk to **Rubha Hanais** at the northern end of the beach and go through the right-hand of two gates; continue across the neck of **Rubha Chràiginis**, go through another gate and descend to **Tràigh Hough**.

Continue along the beach as the tide allows or follow the paths through the edge of the dunes to its rear. Around 750 metres along the beach, where a rocky outcrop crosses the shore, head into the dunes to join a distinct pebble-metalled track and follow it east-north-east away from the shore for 1km.

You're passing through a landscape of low-lying dunes dotted with **abandoned bunkers, emplacements and observation posts** – long-vacant reminders of the military presence on Tiree during the Second World War.

About 100 metres before reaching a cattle grid, leave the track at the foot of the north ridge of **Beinn Hough**, climbing directly south. Pass an observation post and emplacement before reaching the summit triangulation point (119m) which stands next to another observation post. ▶

Continue south from the summit, descend a little then climb a short way to the communications tower on Beinn Mhurstat. Descend the hill along the access road on its western flank. Turn right at the T-junction and continue south-west along the road back towards Sandaig. ▶

Continue along the road for 1.5km through **Sandaig** to rejoin the track leading back to **Tràigh nan Gilean**. Retrace your steps to the gate at the southern end of the beach, go through, then follow the path south-east, climbing for 500 metres before passing through another gate. Descend south to the rear of the dunes behind **Tràigh Bhì**, then retrace your outward route around to the eastern end of **Balephuil Bay**. Go through the gate, climb the grassy slope, go through another gate and turn right onto road. Follow the road south through **West Hynish**, dogleg past the radar station access road and continue past a couple of houses as the road becomes a track. Go through stock gates either side of the last house along the track, pass a sheepfold and go through a final gate. Climb to around 40m and continue east along the coast, soon crossing a dry stone wall and arriving above **Dùn Shiader** once more. From here retrace your outward route to **Hynish**, keeping above the shore to avoid difficult terrain.

There are fine views down to the west coast and east across the island's hinterland.

After 500 metres, the ruins of St Kenneth's Chapel – dating from the late Middle Ages – stand a short way from the road.

APPENDIX A
Route summary table

Walk number	Start	Finish	Distance	Ascent	Time
Rum					
1	Path along the Allt Slugan by Kinloch Castle (NM 402 995)	Kinloch	27km (17 miles); to Dibidil bothy 18.5km (11½ miles); shorter Hallival and Askival route 11km (7 miles)	2025m (6645ft); shorter Hallival and Askival route 1220m (4000ft)	9–10hrs (to Dibidil bothy 6–7hrs); shorter Hallival and Askival route 4½–5½hrs
2	Dibidil bothy (NM 393 927)	Dibidil	10.5km (6.5 miles): The walk in and out from Kinloch adds 8.5km and 3–3½hrs each way	1440m (4720ft)	5–6hrs
3	Around the coast of Rum				
Day 1	Dibidil pony path, between Loch Scresort ferry slipway and Kinloch Castle (NM 404 991)	Dibidil	8.5km (5 miles)	665m (1200ft)	3–3½hrs
Day 2	Dibidil bothy (NM 393 927)	Guirdil	18.5km (11½ miles)	966m (3170ft)	7½–9hrs
Day 3	Guirdil bothy (NG 319 013)	Kinloch	15km (9¼ miles); via Kilmory and Kinloch glens 14km (8¾ miles)	575m (1885ft); via Kilmory and Kinloch glens 395m (1296m)	5½–6½hrs; via Kilmory and Kinloch glens 5–6hrs

Walk number	Start	Finish	Distance	Ascent	Time
4	Kinloch Castle (NM 402 995)	Guirdil	10.5km (6½ miles) each way; via Glen Shellesder: 9.6km (6 miles) each way	415m (1360ft); via Glen Shellesder 296m (970m)	3–3½hrs each way
5	Guirdil bothy (NG 319 013)	Guirdil	9km (5½ miles) to 14.5km (9 miles); walk out back to Kinloch adds 9.5km (6 miles)	708m (2325ft); Bloodstone Hill adds159m (523ft) Ard Nev adds 220m (720ft)	3–3½hrs to 4½–5½hrs; add 3–4hrs for a return to Kinloch
6	Kinloch Castle (NM 402 995)	Kinloch	25.5km (16 miles); shorter alternatives are available	1341m (4402ft); Bloodstone Hill only 907m (2978ft)	Up to 8–9hrs, plus ½hr with ascent of Fionchra
7	Kinloch Castle (NM 402 995)	Kilmory or Harris	Kinloch to Kilmory Bay 16km (10 miles) return; Kinloch to Harris Bay 21.5km (13½ miles) return	Kinloch–Harris Bay 340m (1115ft) each way; Kinloch–Kilmory Bay 185m (607ft) each way	Kinloch to Kilmory Bay 5–5½hrs return; Kinloch to Harris Bay 6–6½hrs return
Eigg					
8	Galmisdale pier (NM 484 838)	Galmisdale	An Sgùrr return 8km (5 miles); An Sgùrr, Grulin and return 11km (7 miles)	540m (1770ft); An Sgùrr return; 393m (1290ft)	An Sgùrr return 3–3½hrs; An Sgùrr, Grulin and return 4–5hrs
9	Galmisdale (NM 484 838); Cleadale to Galmisdale along the coast (NM 477 886)	Cleadale	26km (16 miles); clifftop only route 16.5km (10½ miles); Cleadale to Galmisdale along the coast 14km (8.5 miles)	995m (3265ft), clifftop only route 631m (2070ft); Cleadale to Galmisdale along the coast 457m (1500ft)	8–9hrs; clifftop only route 5–6hrs; Cleadale to Galmisdale along the coast 4–5hrs

Walk number	Start	Finish	Distance	Ascent	Time
Canna					
10	A'Chill (NG 272 053)	A'Chill	20km (12½ miles)	750m (2460ft)	7-8½hrs
11	Bridge linking Canna and Sanday (NG 266 050)	A'Chill	11km (7 miles)	236m (755ft)	3-3½hrs
Muck					
12	Port Mòr (NM 422 794)	Port Mòr	14km (8¾ miles)	442m (1450ft)	4½-5hrs
Coll					
13	Coll Nature Reserve car park (NM 151 538)	Coll RSPB reserve	14.5km (9 miles): 9km (5½ miles) or 12km (7½ miles) with shortcuts	205m (670ft)	4-5hrs, shorter alternatives possible
14	B8071 by Clabhach cottages (GR 181 587)	Clabhach	17km (10½ miles), 13.5km (8½ miles) with shortcut	280m (920ft)	5-6hrs, 4-4½hrs with shortcut
Tiree					
15	Balephetrish Farm, Balephetrish Bay (NM 013 474)	Balephetrish	25km (15½ miles), 13km (8 miles) with shortcut; finishing at Scarinish saves 2.5km	177m (580ft)	6-7hrs, 3-4hrs with shortcut
16	Hynish (NL 985 393)	Hynish	29km (18 miles), shorter variant: 19.5km (12 miles)	686m (2250ft)	7-8hrs, 5-6hrs with shortcut

APPENDIX B

Accommodation

RUM

Visitors should note that at the time of writing the availability of accommodation is in a state of flux (see Rum Introduction) and are advised to check the isle of Rum website well in advance of a visit to see what is available: www.isleofrum.com.

Hostels

Dorm rooms are available at Kinloch Castle's hostel (tel: 01687 462037). At the time of writing a dorm bed costs £16. Exclusive use of dorms requires payment for all beds. Group discounts are available for bookings of 15 or more people. Double and twin rooms cost £45 and 'Oak' rooms with four poster beds £55. Facilities include a public laundry, wireless internet, payphone and Reading Room. At the time of writing there is no bed and breakfast on Rum, but this situation is likely to change in the near future.

Self catering

Currently the only self-catering property for rent on Rum is a three-berth caravan, situated on the shore of Loch Scresort. Contact Fliss on 01687 462744 or email fliss@isleofrum.com.

Camping

The Isle of Rum Community Trust campsite is located on the waterfront between the pier and castle – a 10 minute walk from either. The campsite has toilets, hot showers (£1.50 per shower for non-campers), two wooden camping shelters, picnic benches, taps and washing up basins. Camping costs £5 per adult and £2.50 per child aged 16 and under in summer, £3.50 per adult and £1 per child in winter (showers at castle only).

There are wonderfully located bothies at Dibidil and Guirdil, maintained by the excellent Mountain Bothies Association. MBA bothies are simple shelters, so you need to take your own food, fuel and cooking equipment. You can join the Mountain Bothies Association at www.mountainbothies.org.uk. There is no electricity and the water supply comes from nearby burns (streams). There are no toilets – human waste should be buried away from the bothy and water supplies. Both bothies have a hearth, but driftwood is scarce, especially at Dibidil. Take a tent or bivvy bag with you in case the bothies are busy, which is especially likely in summer.

Wild camping is permitted but please check the Outdoor Access Code for information about your rights and responsibilities (www.outdooraccess-scotland.com). Remember that Rum is a National Nature Reserve so be aware of disturbing wildlife when camping on the island. Please avoid camping near lochans between April and the end of

July to avoid disturbing breeding red throated divers. Camp fires are allowed, away from bird nesting areas, as long as the weather is not too dry and they are kept under control. Places such as Harris and Papadil along the coast, where there's plenty of driftwood, are fine. Light fires at previously used spots to avoid creating too many black holes.

Eigg

Hostels
Glebe Barn Hostel, just over 1km north of the pier, for individuals and groups of up to 24, tel: 01687 482417, www.glebebarn.co.uk.

Bed and breakfast
Lageorna at Cleadale, also has a restaurant and a self catering cottage, tel: 01687 482405, www.lageorna.com.

Tigh an Sithean at Cleadale, bed and breakfast as well as 'camping cocoons' and log cabin, tel: 01687 460049.

Kildonan Farm Guest House, full board accommodation, tel: 01687 482446.

Self-catering
Top House at Cleadale, sleeps up to seven, tel: 01362 668435.

Sandavore Farmhouse, 10mins walk from the pier, sleeps up to eight, tel:01687 482438, www.piercottage.com.

Sandavore Bothy ,very basic and very cheap accommodation for up to four at the foot of the Sgùrr, tel: 01687 482480.

Camping
Eigg Yurts, glamorous camping accommodation for up to six, tel: 01687 460317 or 07811 078747.

More orthodox camping is provided for in a designated area at Cleadale on the north side of the island, tel: 01687 482480.

Canna

Bed and breakfast
Tighard Guest House, on the hillside above the harbour, tel: 0844 93224, www.tighard.com.

Self catering
The Bothy, next door to Gille Brighde, the island's tearoom and restaurant, sleeps four.

Lag nam Boitean is 200m from a beautiful sandy beach and sleeps four, tel: 0844 493 2108, www.nts.org.uk/property.

There is a holiday cottage for rent on Sanday, tel: 01687 462829.

Camping
Wild camping is free of charge but remember to camp away from livestock and beware of disturbing wildlife. The area by Coroghon Mòr is a good spot for a pitch.

Muck

Hotels
Port Mòr House Hotel, near the pier, has eight bedrooms and serves top quality food using locally sourced produce. Full board is available, tel: 01687 462365.

Bed and breakfast
Godag House is 1km north of the harbour and provides full board or B&B, tel: 01687 462371.

Carn Dearg in Port Mòr also provides evening meals if required, tel: 01687 462363.

Self catering
The Isle of Muck estate has four self catering cottages and a yurt, tel: 01687 462362 or email info@isleofmuck.com.

The Bunk House, basic, comfortable accommodation for individuals and groups, tel: 01687 462042. Camping on the island is free but ask at The Craft Shop for good sites.

Coll

Hotels
Coll Hotel, overlooking Arinagour Bay, was voted Scottish island hotel of the year in 2008 and 2009 and has a bar and restaurant, tel: 01879 230334, www.collhotel.com.

Tigh-na-Mara Guest House also overlooks the Bay, tel: 01879 230354, www.tighnamara.info.

Bed and breakfast
B&B is available at The White House on the north-west coast, tel: 01879 230 247.

Self catering
Benmeanach, on the north-west coast beneath Ben Hogh, sleeps five, tel: 01464 821815.

Lonban Cottage, near Breachacha Bay, tel: 01879 230461, www.lonban.co.uk.

Monadh Bhan, by Arinagour, tel: 01879 230362, www.coll-lochoir.co.uk.

Tigh-an-Lochan, near the east end of the island close to Struan Shore, has two double bedrooms, tel: 01879 230395.

First Port of Coll, self-contained flat above the café in Arinagour, sleeps seven, tel: 01879 230488, www.firstportofcoll.com.

Camping
There is a campsite with facilities at Garden House close to Breachacha Beach and Coll airport. The charge is currently £2 per adult and £1 per child, tel: 01879 230374. Wild camping is permitted on the hill behind the hotel; you are requested to ask at the hotel before pitching. There are no facilities.

Tiree

Hotels
Scarinish Hotel, by the old harbour
at Scarinish, tel: 01879 220308,
www.tireescarinishhotel.com.

Tiree Lodge Hotel, overlooking
Gott Bay, tel: 01879 220368.

Hostels
Millhouse Hostel sleeps 16–18 and
Millhouse Farm Hostel sleeps 12, both
are at Cornaig, tel: 01879 220435,
www.tireemillhouse.co.uk.

Bed and Breakfast
Rockvale Guest House, in Balephetrish,
tel: 01879 220 675,
www.rockvaletiree.co.uk.

The Glebe House, by Gott Bay,
tel: 01879 220758.

Kirkapol House, in Kirkapol,
tel: 01879 220729,
www.kirkapoltiree.co.uk.

Cèabhar guest house and restaurant in
Sandaig, tel: 01879 220684,
www.ceabhar.com.

Self catering
A large number of self-catering
properties are available, check the
Isle of Tiree community website
(www.isleoftiree.com).

Camping
Tiree's only campsite is at Balinoe,
booking is advised, tel: 01879 220399.

APPENDIX C
Further reading

Irvine Butterfield, *Dibidil: A Hebridean Adventure*, MBA, 2010.

John L. Campbell, *Canna: The Story of a Hebridean Island*, Birlinn, 2002.

Camille Dressler, *Eigg: The Story of an Island*, Birlinn, 2007.

John Love, *Rum: A Landscape Without Figures*, Birlinn, 2002.

Magnus Magnusson, *Rum: Nature's Island*, Luath, 1997.

The Island of Two Harvests, Tiree and Coll Gaelic Partnership, 2008.

LISTING OF CICERONE GUIDES

Walking – Trekking – Mountaineering – Climbing – Cycling

Over 40 years, Cicerone have built up an outstanding collection of 300 guides, inspiring all sorts of amazing adventures.

 Every guide comes from extensive exploration and research by our expert authors, all with a passion for their subjects. They are frequently praised, endorsed and used by clubs, instructors and outdoor organisations.

All our titles can now be bought as **e-books** and many as iPad and Kindle files and we will continue to make all our guides available for these and many other devices.

Our website shows any **new information** we've received since a book was published. Please do let us know if you find anything has changed, so that we can pass on the latest details. On our **website** you'll also find some great ideas and lots of information, including sample chapters, contents lists, reviews, articles and a photo gallery.

It's easy to keep in touch with what's going on at Cicerone, by getting our monthly **free e-newsletter**, which is full of offers, competitions, up-to-date information and topical articles. You can subscribe on our home page and also follow us on **Facebook** and **Twitter**, as well as our **blog**.

Cicerone – the very best guides for exploring the world.

CICERONE

2 Police Square Milnthorpe Cumbria LA7 7PY
Tel: 015395 62069 info@cicerone.co.uk
www.cicerone.co.uk